mustsees
Boston

Custom House Tower / ©Chee-Onn Leong/Dreamstime.com

LIN

mustsees **Boston**

Editorial Director	Cynthia Clayton Ochterbeck
Editorial Manager	Gwen Cannon
Contributing Writers	Gwen Cannon, Anne-Marie Scott, Carey Sweet
Production Manager	Natasha G. George
Cartography	Peter Wrenn
Photo Editor	Nicole D. Jordan
Proofreader	David G. Cannon
Layout	Natasha G. George, Nicole D. Jordan
Interior Design	Chris Bell, cbdesign
Cover Design	Chris Bell, cbdesign, Natasha G. George

Contact Us

Michelin Travel and Lifestyle North America
One Parkway South
Greenville, SC 29615, USA
travel.lifestyle@us.michelin.com
www.michelintravel.com

Michelin Travel Partner
Hannay House
39 Clarendon Road
Watford, Herts WD17 1JA, UK
www.ViaMichelin.com
travelpubsales@uk.michelin.com

Special Sales

For information regarding bulk sales, customized
editions and premium sales, please contact us at:
travel.lifestyle@us.michelin.com
www.michelintravel.com

Michelin Travel Partner
Société par actions simplifiées au capital de 11 288 880 EUR
27 cours de l'Île Seguin - 92100 Boulogne Billancourt (France)
R.C.S. Nanterre 433 677 721

© Michelin Travel Partner
ISBN 978-2-067190-41-2
Printed: March 2014
Printed and bound in Italy

Note to the reader:
While every effort is made to ensure that all information printed in this guide is correct
and up-to-date, Michelin Travel Partner accepts no liability for any direct, indirect or
consequential losses howsoever caused so far as such can be excluded by law. Admission
prices listed for sights in this guide are for a single adult, unless otherwise specified.

© Gwer: Camoni/Michelin

Boston skyline

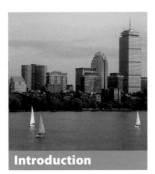

Introduction

Boston: Grounded in History 22

p 48

p 64

TABLE OF CONTENTS

★★★ ATTRACTIONS

Unmissable attractions awarded three stars in this guide include:

Isabella Stewart Gardner Museum p 56

Courtesy of Nic Lehoux

Museum of Fine Arts, Boston p 58

©Museum of Fine Arts, Boston

New England Aquarium p 81

© S. Cheng/New England Aquarium

MUST KNOW

Cape Cod National Seashore p 117
©Lillian Britten/iStockphoto.com

Boston Children's Museum p 78
©Oscar Williams/Boston Children's Museum

Harvard University p 36
©Jorge Salcedo/iStockphoto.com

Peabody Essex Museum p 109
/sylvania/
Museum

Faneuil Hall p 48
©Photo168/Dreamstime.com

★★★ ATTRACTIONS

Unmissable sights in and around Boston

For more than 75 years people have used the Michelin stars to take the guesswork out of travel. Our star-rating system helps you make the best decision on where to go, what to do, and what to see.

★★★	Unmissable
★★	Worth a trip
★	Worth a detour
No star	Recommended

MUST KNOW

ACTIVITIES

Unmissable Boston tours, sports events and more
Boston is a thriving year-round mecca for those seeking entertainment, amusement, inspiration and relaxation. We recommend every activity in this guide, but the Michelin Man highlights our top picks.

 ## For Kids

Bowling at Cape Ann Lanes *p 104*
Duckling Day Parade *p 84*
Flying Horses Carousel
  (Martha's Vineyard) *p 121*
Freeman Farm *p 103/104*
Giant Ocean Tank at the New
  England Aquarium *p 81*
Ice Skating on Frog Pond *p 73*
Museum of Fine Arts, family
  programs *p 59*
Puppet Showplace Theatre *p 79*
Children's Museum Shop at the
  Boston Children's Museum *p 79*
Swan Boats at the Public
  Garden *p 80*

 ## Outdoors

Blue Hills Reservation *p 77*
Chinatown Park *p 69*
Mount Auburn Cemetery *p 54*
Wachusett Mountain *p 71*
Whale Watching *p 72*
Wompatuck State Park *p 77*

 ## Focus on History

Freedom Trail Foundation
  Tours *p 43*
Reading of the Declaration of
  Independence *p 47*
Battle of Bunker Hill Museum *p 45*

 ## Experience the Arts

Boston Philharmonic pre-concert
  lectures *p 89*
Boston Pops summer concerts *p 88*
Colonial Theatre *p 88*

Concerts on the Esplanade *p 70*
Fort Point Arts Community
  Art Walk *p 35*
Society of Arts and Crafts on
  Newbury Street *p 92*
Yin Yu Tang House at Peabody
  Essex Museum (Salem) *p 111*

 ## Sporting Events

Boston Marathon *p 75*
Cape Cod Baseball Leagues *p 115*
Head of the Charles Regatta *p 75*
Red Sox Game at Fenway Park *p 72*

 ## Shopping

Food Stalls at Quincy Market *p 91*
Haymarket *p 93*
in-jean-ius *p 95*
North End eateries *p 31*
Riccardi *p 95*
Salmagundi *p 95*

 ## Nightlife

The Beehive *p 96*
Bin 26 Enoteca *p 96*
Howl at the Moon *p 97*
Paradise Rock Club *p 99*

 ## Day's Out

Boston Harborfest *p 75*
Boston Flower & Garden Show *p 68*
Feast Days in the
  North End *p 75*
Boston Pops Fireworks
  Spectacular *p 70*

STAR ATTRACTIONS

CALENDAR OF EVENTS

Listed below is a selection of the Boston area's most popular annual events. Please note that dates may change from year to year. For more detailed information, call the Greater Boston Convention & Visitors Bureau at 888-733-2678. On the Web visit www.bostonusa.com or www.cityofboston.gov/calendar.

January

Chinese New Year
(late Jan or early Feb)
617-635-4447
Chinatown
www.cityofboston.gov/calendar

Winter Carnival
Harvard Square, Cambridge
617-491-3434
www.harvardsquare.com

Boston Wine Festival
617-330-9355
Boston Harbor Hotel
www.bostonwinefest.net

February

Lunar New Year Festival
978-745-9500
Peabody Essex Museum, Salem
www.pem.org

Chocolate and Ice
Sculpture Festival
978-465-6555
Salem
http://northofboston.org

Hasty Pudding Theatricals
617-495-5205
12 Holyoke St., Harvard
University, Cambridge
http://hastypudding.org

March

Boston Flower & Garden Show
617-933-4900
Bayside Exposition Center
www.masshort.org

St. Patrick's Day Parade
781-436-3377
West Broadway St., South Boston
www.southbostonparade.org

April

Boston Marathon
617-236-1652
Hopkinton to Boston
www.baa.org

Boston Red Sox Opening Day
877-733-7699
Fenway Park, 4 Yawkey Way, Back Bay
http://boston.redsox.mbl.com

Nantucket Daffodil Festival
508-228-1700
Various locations, Nantucket
www.nantucketchamber.org

Patriots' Day
781-862-2480
Lexington and Concord
http://lexingtonchamber.org

Arts First Festival
617-495-8676
Harvard University, Cambridge
http://ofa.fas.harvard.edu

May

Beacon Hill Hidden
Gardens Tour
617-227-4392
Beacon Hill
www.beaconhillgardenclub.org

Cape Cod Maritime Days
508-362-3225
Various locations
www.capecodmaritimedays.com

Duckling Day
617-723-8144
Boston Common
friendsofthepublicgarden.org

Kite Festival
617-953-5315
Franklin Park, Dorchester
www.cityofboston.gov/parks

MUST KNOW

June

Dragon Boat Festival
Charles River near Harvard
University, Cambridge
www.bostondragonboat.org
**Provincetown International
Film Festival**
Various locations, Provincetown
www.ptownfilmfest.org
North End Italian Feast Days
(Jun–early Sept)
North End, Boston
www.northendboston.com

July

Boston Harborfest
617-227-1528
Boston Harbor and City Hall Plaza
www.bostonharborfest.com
**Boston Pops Fireworks
Spectacular**
Hatch Shell at The Esplanade
www.july4th.org
Annual 4th of July Carnival
Hastings Park, Lexington
www.lexingtonlions.org

August

Salem Maritime Festival
978-740-1652
Historic Waterfront, Salem
www.nps.gov/sama
August Moon Festival
617-350-6303
Chinatown
www.chinatownmainstreet.org
**Boston Antique & Classic
Boat Festival**
617-666-8530
Hawthorne Cove Marina,
10 White St., Salem
www.by-the-sea.com
Dine Out Boston
888-733-2678
Various locations
www.bostonusa.com

September

Boston Arts Festival
617-635-3911
Christopher Columbus Park,
Waterfront
www.bostonusa.com
Cambridge Carnival International
617-863 0476
Kendall Square, Cambridge
www.cambridgecarnival.org

October

Haunted Happenings
978-744-3663
Various locations, Salem
www.hauntedhappenings.org
Head of the Charles Regatta
617-868-6200
Charles River, Cambridge
www.hocr.org
Oktoberfest in Harvard Square
617-491-3434
Harvard Square, Cambridge
www.harvardsquare.com

November

Boston Antiquarian Book Fair
617-266-6540
Hynes Convention Center
www.bostonbookfair.com
**Thanksgiving at
Plimoth Plantation**
508-746-1622
Plimoth Plantation, Plymouth
www.plimoth.org

December

Enchanted Village
866-856-7326
Jordan's Furniture,
100 Stockwell Dr., Avon
www.jordans.com
First Night Boston
857-600-1590
Various locations
www.firstnightboston.org

CALENDAR OF EVENTS

PRACTICAL INFORMATION

WHEN TO GO

Boston offers year-round incentives for a visit, but most tourists descend upon the city from May through October. The summer stretch brims with sun-drenched concerts, cruises and cafes and, in late August, the excitement of college students, both new and returning, moving into dorms, apartments and starting classes. In early October, heat and humidity give way to crisp, dry air, when trees burst with color, and hotels overflow with guests; it's also the month that all eyes turn to the Charles River for the world's largest two-day rowing event. The surge levels out by late October, when cool weather and lower room rates provide a window of opportunity for savvy visitors. Come November, winter light casts a cozy glow on red brick around the city, as holiday shopping—and often, snow—keep the hustle and bustle indoors. But if you love winter sports, there's plenty of outdoor action to be had in and around Boston. Freezing temperatures remain through February, but March welcomes the first signs of spring with temperatures in the 50s (March and November are among the rainiest months). Sightseers of a different breed pack the city in April for Patriots' Day and the Boston Marathon. But, for many visitors, the biggest draw of the year comes with July 4, when Boston puts on a big show celebrating its pivotal role in American independence.

KNOW BEFORE YOU GO

Before you go, contact the following tourist organizations.

Greater Boston Convention and Visitors Bureau

2 Copley Place, Suite 105, Boston, MA 02116. 617-536-4100 or 888-733-2678; www.bostonusa.com.

Cambridge Tourism Office

4 Brattle Street, Cambridge, MA 02138. 617-441-2884 or 800-862-5678; www.cambridge-usa.org.

Cape Cod Welcome Center

5 Patti Page Way (Rte 6 & Rte 132), Centerville, MA 02601. 508-362-3225 or 888-332-2732. www.capecodchamber.com.

Seasonal Temperatures in Boston

	Jan	Apr	July	Oct
Avg. high	36°F/2°C	54°F/12°C	80°F/27°C	62°F/17°C
Avg. Low	20°F/-7°C	38°F/3°C	63°F/17°C	46°F/8°C

Websites

Here are some additional websites to help you plan your trip:
- www.boston-online.com • www.massvacation.com
- www.citysearch.com (lists entertainment and restaurant reviews)
- http://chowhound.chow.com (restaurant recommendations of local foodies)

Safety Tips

Visitors should remember these common-sense tips to ensure a safe and enjoyable visit:

- After dark, avoid visiting the Boston Common and other wooded areas.
- Steer clear of secluded streets and alleyways, even in pretty neighborhoods.
- Stay awake when riding public transportation. Avoid empty subway cars and deserted station hallways and platforms after 9pm.
- Keep a firm hold on purses and knapsacks.
- Don't use ATM machines on secluded streets late at night.

Massachusetts Office of Travel & Tourism

10 Park Plaza, Ste. 4510, Boston.
617-973-8500 or 800-227-6277.
www.massvacation.com.

Boston Common Visitor Center

139 Tremont St., Boston.
617-426-3115. Open Mon–Fri
8:30am–5pm, Sat–Sun 9am–5pm.

Prudential Visitor Information Booth

Center Court of Prudential Center,
800 Boylston St. 617 867-8389.
Open Mon–Fri 8:30am–5:30pm,
Sat–Sun 10am–6pm.

National Park Visitor Centers

Faneuil Hall: 617-242-5642;
www.nps.gov/bost. Open year-round daily 9am–6pm. Closed Jan
1, Thanksgiving Day & Dec 25.
Charlestown Navy Yard: 617-242-5601. Open Jul–Sept daily
9am–6pm; rest of year call
for hours.

International Visitors

Visitors from outside the US can obtain information from the Greater Boston Convention & Visitors Bureau *(888-733-2678; www.bostonusa.com)* or from the US embassy or consulate in their country of residence. For a list of American consulates and embassies abroad, visit the US State Department Bureau listing on the Internet at: http://travel.state.gov.

Entry Requirements

Travelers entering the United States under the Visa Waiver Program (VWP) must have a machine-readable **passport**. Any traveler without a machine readable passport will be required to obtain a visa before entering the US. Citizens of VWP countries are permitted to enter the US for general business or tourist purposes for a maximum of 90 days without needing a visa. Requirements for the Visa Waiver Program can be found at the Department of State's Visa Services website *(http://travel.state.gov)*. All citizens of nonparticipating countries must have a visitor's visa. Upon entry, nonresident foreign visitors must present a valid passport and round-trip transportation ticket. Canadian citizens are also now required to have documents to establish citizenship; a valid passport is recommended.

US Customs

All articles brought into the US must be declared at the time of entry. Prohibited items: plant material; firearms and ammunition (if not for sports); meat or poultry products. For information, contact

MASSACHUSETTS BAY TRANSPORTATION AUTHORITY RAPID TRANSIT/ KEY BUS ROUTES MAP

US Customs, 1300 Pennsylvania Ave. NW, Washington, DC 20229 *(877-277-5511; www.cbp.gov)*.

Driving in the US

Visitors bearing a valid driver's license issued by their country of residence are not required to obtain an International Driver's License. Drivers must carry vehicle registration and/or rental contract, and proof of automobile insurance at all times. Gasoline is sold by the gallon (1 gal=3.8 liters). Drive on the right-hand side of the road.

Time Zone

Boston is in the **Eastern Standard Time (EST)** zone, 3 hours ahead of Los Angeles and 5 hours behind Greenwich Mean Time.

GETTING THERE
By Air

Both domestic and international flights service **Logan International Airport (BOS)**, located 2 miles northeast of downtown (for points north, take Rte. 1A south to the Sumner Tunnel and I-93 north; for points west, take the Ted Williams Tunnel to I-90 westbound Masspike; for points south, take the Ted Williams to I-90 west exit 24 *(800-235-6426; www.massport.com/logan-airport)*.

Shuttles

A free shuttle-bus service between terminals is available and runs daily. Call or visit the airport website for schedules. A number of companies offer transport from the airport to downtown hotels by **shared van**, which averages $16 each. **Water taxis** *(see sidebar below)* also service Logan airport.

Subway

See map above. MBTA's Blue and
Silver lines are the most-budget
friendly options to get to and from
Logan. *See By Bus for free rides.*

Airport Taxis and Shuttles

A metered taxi service from the
airport to Boston-area hotels
costs $25–$35. For Boston taxi
companies servicing the airport:

Boston Water Taxi

Experience taxi service via boat. Massport courtesy bus service runs from the
arrival terminals directly to the Logan dock; from there, hop aboard the MBTA
Harbor Express, which offers a full schedule of daily connections between
Logan, Long Wharf and the South Shore. Vessels are wheelchair accessible.
For schedules and rates, 617-222-6999 or www.massport.com.

www.mass.gov. For shuttles to and from Logan: www.massport.com.

By Train

Amtrak trains leave from South Station Downtown *(Atlantic Ave. & Summer St.; 800-872-7245; www.amtrak.com).* Suburban MBTA trains depart from South Station and North Station *(135 Causeway St.),* North End. Schedules and fares: 617-222-3200; www.mbta.com.

By Bus

Boston's main bus terminal is located at South Station *(617-222-3200).* To and from Logan airport, the Silver Line **bus is free** to the Red line at South Station; one way takes about 30min. For fares, schedules and routes, 800-231-2222; www.greyhound.com.

By Car

Boston can be accessed from major highways: I-95 circumvents the city on the west, I-90 enters from the west, and I-93 forms the north–south corridor through the city.

GETTING AROUND
By Car

If you have the choice, don't drive in Boston. Downtown streets weave, wind and end, according to no set or sane pattern. Street signs may change from block to block: Winter turns into Summer, Court into State, Kneeland into Stuart. If you must drive in Boston, avoid commuter rush hours (weekdays 7:30am–9am and 4pm–6pm). A car is great for visiting the surrounding areas as well as Cape Cod. Use of seat belts is required. Child safety seats are mandatory for children ages 4 and under or 40lbs or less.

Parking

Street parking is generally difficult to find, adding another deterrent to driving in Boston. If you decide to brave the roads, garages at **Boston Common**, **John Hancock Tower** and **Prudential Center** are all operational 24 hours a day. Rates run the gamut from $8/hour to $39/day; some facilities give "early-bird" discounts (25 percent) for parking before 10:30am.

Important Phone Numbers	
Emergency police/ambulance/fire (24hrs)	**911**
Police (non-emergency, Mon–Fri 9am–6pm)	617-343-4200
Poison Control	617-232-2120
Physician Referral	617-726-5800
Dental Emergencies	508-651-3521
24-hour Pharmacies	
CVS – 587 Boylston St., Back Bay, Boston	617-437-8414
36 White St., Cambridge	617-876-5519
Family Aid Boston	617-542-7286
Weather	508-822-0634

On Foot

Walking is one of the best ways to explore Boston. With the Central Artery out of the way *(see Big Dig in Landmarks)*, it's easy to stroll all over town. Some of the best walking neighborhoods include the Back Bay, Beacon Hill, Downtown and the North End.

By Public Transportation

The **Massachusetts Bay Transportation Authority (MBTA)** operates a network of subways (known locally as the "T") buses and elevated trains *(617-222-3200; www.mbta.com)*.

MBTA Commuter Rail Line – The MBTA also links Boston with surrounding towns and cities, including Providence, Worcester, Concord, Plymouth and other cities.

Subway – A combination of walking and taking the T is the ideal way to get around Boston and Cambridge. At just $2 per ride, the subway (metro) will take you to almost every section of both (though it's rarely a direct line between any two points).

Buy your ticket at station vending machines. A 7-day unlimited ride pass costs $18.

By Taxi

Cabs are readily available at all hours in Boston; you can hail cabs on the street, or find them outside major hotels. Caution: use only cabs showing a "Boston Licensed Taxi" medallion. Rates within the city start at $2.60, then 40¢ for each additional one-seventh of a mile. If you plan to travel to or from the airport or suburbs, flat rates apply outside the 12-mile downtown radius. Passengers pay some roadway and tunnel charges *(see http://bpdnews.com/taxi-rates)*. Major cab companies include:

Ambassador Brattle Cab – 617-492-1100; www.ambassadorbrattle.com.

Boston Cab – 617-536-5010.

City Cab – 617-536-5100.

Top Cab – 617-266-4800.

For a wheelchair-accessible van, contact **Metro Cab** at 617-782-5500 or www.boston-cab.com.

ACCESSIBILITY
Disabled Travelers

Federal law requires that businesses (including hotels and restaurants) provide access for the disabled, devices for the hearing impaired, and designated parking spaces. For information, contact the Society for Accessible Travel and Hospitality (SATH), 347 Fifth Ave., Suite 605, New York NY 10016 *(212-447-7284; http://sath.org)*. All national parks have facilities

PRACTICAL INFORMATION

for the disabled, and offer free or discounted passes. For details, contact the National Park Service *(Office of Public Inquiries, Washington, DC; 202-208-4747; www.nps.gov)*. Passengers who will need assistance with train or bus travel should give advance notice to Amtrak *(800-872-7245 or 800-523-6590TDD/TTY; www.amtrak.com)* or Greyhound *(800-752-4841 or 800-345-3109TDD/TTY; www.greyhound.com)*. Reservations for hand-controlled rental cars should be made in advance with the rental company.

Local Sources

For information about disabled access to public transportation, contact the Massachusetts Bay Transportation Authority: 617-222-3200 or 800-392-6100; www.mbta.com. The following agencies also provide detailed information.
Boston Center for Independent Living – 60 Temple Pl. 617-338-6665. www.bostoncil.org.
Massachusetts Office on Disability – 1 Ashburton Pl. 617-727-7440 or 800-322-2020/TTY. www.mass.gov.

ACCOMMODATIONS

For suggested accommodations, see Must Stay at the back of the guide.

An area visitors' guide including a lodging directory is available (free) from the Greater Boston Convention and Visitors Bureau *(see p12)*. Check its website *(www.bostonusa.com)* for discount-reservation services offering the best rates in the city, and direct links to most of the hotels and B&Bs. You can make reservations online, too.

Hotel Reservation Services

National hotel booking sites: www.expedia.com; www.hotels.com; www.orbitz.com.
Local agencies include:
B&B Agency of Boston – 800-248-9262; www.boston-bnbagency.com.
Boston Hotels – 800-478-3930; www.bostonhotels.travel.
Bed & Breakfast Associates – 888-486-6018; http://bnbboston.com
Host Homes of Boston – 617-244-1308, (out of state 800-600-1308); http://hosthomesofboston.com.

Hostels

A no-frills, inexpensive alternative to hotels, hostels are a good choice for budget travelers. A bed in a dorm-style room costs $40–$55 per night. Private rooms are $130–$200 per night. For

---

And Toto Too

Numerous New England hotels throw down the red carpet for their VIP (Very Important Pet) guests. Kimpton Hotels, a boutique chain with properties in Boston and Cambridge, makes a special point of welcoming Fido and Fluffy along. At the Onyx Hotel (155 Portland St.), pets are playfully greeted, given treats and adorned with a leopard-print collar tag. Fido's birthday? The Hotel Marlowe in Cambridge *(see Must Stay)* will order a cake from Polka Dog Bakery, which specializes in pet goodies. At both hotels (along with sister property Nine Zero Hotel), the staff can even set up pet-sitting and pet-walking services for you.

Measurement Equivalents									
Degrees Fahrenheit	95°	86°	77°	68°	59°	50°	41°	32°	23°	14°
Degrees Celsius	35°	30°	25°	20°	15°	10°	5°	0°	-5°	-10°

1 inch = 2.54 centimeters
1 mile = 1.6 kilometers
1 quart = 0.9 liters

1 foot = 30.5 centimeters
1 pound = 0.45 kilograms
1 gallon = 3.8 liters

more information about hostels in Boston, contact Hostelling International, Boston, 19 Stuart St. 617-536-9455. http://bostonhostel.org. Hostels are also available around Cape Cod, including Martha's Vineyard and Nantucket (www.hiusa.org or call 240-650-2100).

COMMUNICATIONS
Area Codes
To call between different area codes, dial 1 + area code + seven-digit number. The same applies to local calls, even within the same area code.
Boston & Cambridge: **617** and **857**
Boston Suburbs: **339** and **781**
Outlying Areas: **508** and **774** (SW); **351** and **978** (NW).
Cape Cod, Nantucket and Martha's Vineyard: **508**

Internet Access
Boston is a hi-tech town but wireless Internet access often comes at a price. The city's better hotels often charge $10 or more per day for Internet access. To find places to plug into the Web free of charge, visit www.wififreespot.com. It offers a reasonably up-to-date list of locations that offer free Wi-Fi around Boston—and all of Massachusetts—including coffee houses, restaurants, parks, hotels and more. Or use the public computers at the Boston Public Library's central branch. For

In the News
The best way to find out what's happening while you're in town is to check the local newspapers: Boston's biggest dailies are the *Boston Globe* (www.bostonglobe.com) and *Boston Herald* (http://bostonherald.com); the weekly alternative paper is *The Phoenix* (http://thephoenix.com). For a guide to the city's top shops, services, and much more, check out *Boston* magazine's annual Best of Boston list (www.bostonmagazine.com).

information on hours and rules of use, visit www.bpl.org.

Newspapers
Boston's biggest dailies, the *Boston Globe* and the *Boston Herald,* are available at newsstands and stores around the city. The free weekly alternative newspaper, *The Phoenix*, is easily accessible at boxes on many Boston streets and at some coffee houses and restaurants. For selection of international newspapers, no store in the Boston area beats Out of Town News in Harvard Square in Cambridge *(Sun–Thu 6am–10pm, Fri–Sat 6am–11pm).*

DISCOUNTS
For a Price
The following offer discounts on Boston-area attractions:

CityPass – *$51; $36 children ages 3–11; good for nine days from first use.* Includes a ticket for each of the following: Museum of Science, New England Aquarium, Skywalk Observatory, Museum of Fine Arts, as well as Harvard Museum of Natural History or Old State House. Available for purchase at **Greater Boston Convention & Visitors Bureau**, participating attractions, or online at www.citypass.com. The program also helps you save time; CityPass users may be able to skip lines at some attractions.

Go Boston Card – *1, 2, 3, 5 and 7 day cards available; $54.99–$194.99.* Present the Go Boston card at any of the participating attractions, tour companies, restaurants and shops. Discount varies per activity. Order by phone at 866-628-9027 or online at www.smartdestinations.com.

Free

Boston USA Specials – *Free. Print coupons from www.bostonusa.com.* Check the website for individual coupons good for tours, tickets and much more.

For Families

Family-Friendly Value PASS – *Free. Print the pass at www.bostonusa.com.* This pass, from the **Greater Boston Convention and Visitors Bureau**, provides families with discounts to more than 70 attractions, restaurants and shops.

For Senior Citizens

Many hotels, attractions and restaurants offer discounts to visitors age 62 or older (proof of age may be required). **AARP** (formerly American Association of Retired Persons) offers discounts to its members *(601 E St. NW, Washington, DC 20049; 888-687-2277; www.aarp.com).*

ELECTRICITY

Voltage in the US is 120 volts AC, 60 Hz. Foreign-made appliances may need AC adapters (available at specialty travel and electronics stores) and North American flat-blade plugs.

MONEY AND CURRENCY EXCHANGE

The easiest way to get **cash** in Boston is with your personal ATM or debit card at an automated teller machine (ATM), at banks, as well as some hotels and stores. Exchange currency in Back Bay at **Bank of America** *(699 Boylston St.; 617-262-0544; www.bankofamerica.com; open Mon–Fri 9am–6pm, Sat 10am–5pm),* and downtown at **Citizens Bank** *(28 State St. at Congress St.; 617-725-5900; www.citizensbank.com; open Mon–Thu 8:30am–5pm, Fri 8:30am–6pm, Sat 9am–noon.* **American Express Travel Service** in Boston is Altour *(155 Federal St., 617-439-4400; www.americanexpress.com; open Mon–Fri 8:30am–5pm).* **Travelex** has a Boston office *(745 Boylston St., 617-266-7560; www.travelex.com; open Mon–Fri 9am–7pm, Sat 10am–6pm, Sun noon–5pm).*

For cash transfers, **Western Union** *(800-225-5227; www.westernunion. com)* has agents throughout Boston. Banks and a few other businesses might accept travelers' checks with photo identification. To report lost or stolen credit cards: **American Express** *(866-465-4205)* **MasterCard** *(800-627-8372)* **Visa** *(800-847-2911).*

MUST KNOW

OPENING HOURS

General hours for businesses and services in Boston and the area:
Banks 9am–5pm.
Bars close 2am.
Stores 9am–8pm.
Post Office 8am–5pm.
Spas Mon–Fri 9am–9pm, Sat–Sun 9am–6pm.

SMOKING

Like most major American cities, Boston has turned a cold eye on smoking in public places. Restaurants, bars and other public venues are smoke free, as are most hotels in the city—and most impose a hefty deep-cleaning fee for guests who choose to smoke in their rooms.

SPECTATOR SPORTS

With the Red Sox winning the 2004, 2007 and 2013 World Series; the New England Patriots taking the 2004 and 2005 Super Bowl trophies (along with the 2007 AFC title); and the Boston Celtics picking up the 2008 NBA Championship, loyal Boston fans have a lot to crow about. While the Red Sox have been slugging away in the legendary Fenway Park *(see For Fun)* for nearly 100 years, **the Celtics and Bruins got new digs,** TD Garden, in 1995. (Even Bostonians who still mourn the loss of the old Boston Garden will admit that it was far from a comfortable place to watch a game.) Both the New England Patriots and the New England Revolution also play in a newer stadium, Gillette Stadium, erected in 2002 In Foxborough, MA, about 24 miles outside of Boston.

TAXES AND TIPPING

Prices displayed in Massachusetts do not include the state sales tax of 6.25 percent, which is not reimbursable. It is customary to give a small gift of money—a **tip**— for services rendered, to waitstaff (15–20 percent of bill), porters ($1–$2 per bag), chamber maids ($1–$5 per day) and cab drivers (15 percent of fare).

Spectator Sports			
Season	**Venue**	**Phone**	**Website**
Baseball	**Boston Red Sox**		
Apr–Oct	Fenway Park	877-733-7699	boston.redsox.mbl.com
Hockey	**Boston Bruins**		
Oct–Apr	TD Garden	617-624-2327	http://bruinsnhl.com
Football	**New England Patriots**		
Sept–Jan	Gillette Stadium	800-543-1776	www.patriots.com
Basketball	**Boston Celtics**		
Nov–Apr	TD Garden	866-423-5849	www.nba.com/celtics
Soccer	**New England Revolution**		
Apr–Oct	Gillette Stadium	508-543-8200	www.revolutionsoccer.net

GROUNDED IN HISTORY

The reflections of buildings—some up to three centuries old—on the exteriors of Boston's glass skyscrapers are the ultimate display of the city's elegant melding of old and new. Around Boston, sleek towers of commerce and government showcase the city's role as the administrative and financial hub of New England. University buildings, museums, and concert halls mark it as a center of learning and culture. Yet, history is at its core. Reminders of Boston's importance as the hotbed of American independence are visible everywhere. Whether you spend two days or two weeks in Boston, you'll return home with stories and photos that bring together hundreds of bygone years.

Boston Brahmins

The "proper Bostonian," or Brahmin, descends from New England's early Puritan settlers who shared a common language and culture, and whose close-knit society set Boston apart by the 19C as the city where "the Lowells talk only to the Cabots, and the Cabots talk only to God." Stereotyped as refined, conservative and Harvard-educated, the proper Bostonian today represents an ever-decreasing percentage of the city's population.

In 1630 about 700 Puritans arrived on the coast of Massachusetts to establish a settlement for the **Massachusetts Bay Company**. They named their new colony after the English town many of them hailed from, Boston. Because of its maritime commerce and shipbuilding, Boston quickly became the largest town in the British colonies. Early on, the Puritans focused on education, which is still a centerpiece of Boston life. The first public school in America (c.1630) and the first college in the colonies (Harvard College, 1636—now **Harvard University**) were founded in Boston. (Today there are nearly 70 colleges in the metropolitan area.) Boston's pivotal role in history was cemented in the late 1700s after the British parliament levied high

Back Bay

© Armin Sepp/Fotolia.com

Statue of Paul Revere

©Julia Freeman-Woolpert/iStockphoto.com

taxes and harsh trade regulations against the colonies to pay for the costly French and Indian War. The colonists, who were still British citizens, claimed their rights to representation were being denied. Support for British rule continued to erode with the events of March 5, 1770, the date of the **Boston Massacre**. On that day, Bostonians and Redcoats clashed outside the State House. Several British soldiers loaded their weapons and fired, killing five men.

Three years later, the **Boston Tea Party** aggravated the situation further. A tax on tea so angered colonists that they refused to allow the East India Company to unload its ships. On December 16, 1773, a group of Bostonians, disguised as Mohawk Indians, boarded the ships and dumped the tea into Boston Harbor.

In April 1775, General Thomas Gage sent 700 British soldiers to **Lexington** and **Concord** *(see Excursions)* to arrest Patriot leaders and seize their weapons. The sexton of Old North Church *(see Landmarks)* hung two lanterns in the bell tower to signal the Redcoats' departure by boat, and **Paul Revere** made his famous midnight ride to Lexington. There, the first shots of the Revolutionary War were fired. The war lasted eight years. The Treaty of Paris was signed on September 3, 1783. Soon enough, Boston was established as one of America's great cultural and educational centers, a reputation that, justifiably, persists. The city became a gathering place for intellectuals and writers, and well-heeled Bostonians donated their personal collections of art and artifacts to create some of the museums that we still visit today.

Boston Fast Facts

City population: 636,500
Area: 48.6 square miles
Miles of coastline: 43
Number of college students: 250,000 (one of every 10 residents in Greater Boston)
Biggest mistake visitors make: bringing a car into Boston proper
Second biggest mistake visitors make: attempting to imitate a Boston accent

BOSTON, MASSACHUSETTS

NEIGHBORHOODS

Boston may be small by big-city standards, but it packs a lot of personality into its compact 43 square miles. It remains a city of neighborhoods, each with its own character, style and vibe. Some feel more grown-up, while others are decidedly collegiate. You can go from one neighborhood to the next in short order—if you're not driving! Remember, in Boston it's best to walk or take the "T" (subway).

Charles River Basin and skyline of Back Bay

© Greater Boston CVB/FayFoto, Inc.

Touring Tip

Back Bay's east end near the Public Garden has the most upscale shops (think Brooks Brothers, Zegna, Armani, Cartier) and the area's finest residences. The farther you roam west toward Massachusetts Avenue, the less exclusive it becomes. The Kenmore Square area attracts a mixed crowd of students and young urban dwellers to its funky shops and bookstores. South of the fast-paced Boylston Street corridor, Back Bay takes on a dramatically different appearance. Here, buildings of cement and steel, such as the Prudential Center and Copley Place *(see Shopping)* and the Christian Science Center *(see p26)*, create a decidedly 20C scale and flavor.

HISTORIC QUARTERS

Back Bay★★

It's the place the fashionable shop, the trendy dine, the well-off live—and everyone else watches. Built on a landfill centuries ago, Back Bay, bordered by the Charles River, the Public Garden and Huntington and Massachusetts avenues, is one of Boston's most expensive and elegant neighborhoods. Intermingled with towering churches and 20C high rises, stately rows of historic brownstones and bowfront buildings flank wide Parisian-style boulevards. Stroll the streets chock-a-block full with shops, spas, galleries, restaurants, sidewalk cafes, and some of the most expensive real estate in the city.

Top Three Things to Do in Back Bay

Shop Newbury Street★★

Eight-block-long Newbury Street starts at the Ritz-Carlton Hotel on Arlington Street and ends on Massachusetts Avenue—with scores of designer boutiques, top-brand names and funky shops in between *(see Shopping)*. Best of all, if you decide to totally overhaul your fashion style with a shopping splurge, you can stop in to one of Newbury's numerous salons to complete the look.

Gawk at the Architecture

Along Commonwealth Avenue and Newbury, Marlborough and Beacon streets, the early residential buildings reflect contemporary French tastes—the omnipresent mansard roof and the controlled building height are dead giveaways. The buildings look like they've owned the land forever—it's pretty amazing considering

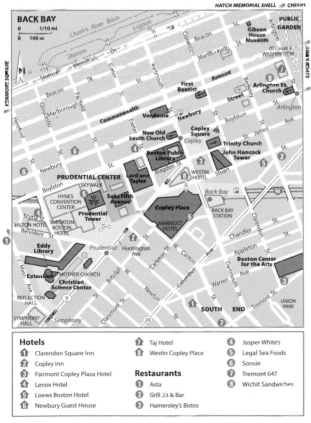

Hotels

1. Clarendon Square Inn
2. Copley Inn
3. Fairmont Copley Plaza Hotel
4. Lenox Hotel
5. Loews Boston Hotel
6. Newbury Guest House
7. Taj Hotel
8. Westin Copley Place

Restaurants

1. Asta
2. Grill 23 & Bar
3. Hamersley's Bistro
4. Jasper White's
5. Legal Sea Foods
6. Sonsie
7. Tremont 647
8. Wichit Sandwiches

NEIGHBORHOODS

that, until the late 1850s there wasn't even any land there. What is now Newbury was then part of Boston Harbor. Post-1870s buildings west of Dartmouth Street showcase prevailing revival styles (such as Gothic, Richardsonian Romanesque and Georgian).

Go to Church

Back Bay is dotted with pretty churches, but three stand out. The 1861 **Arlington Street Church** (Arlington St. at Boylston St.) is famous for its 16 steeple bells—and Tiffany windows. **Trinity Church**★★ (see Landmarks) is recognizable by its massive central tower. And **First Baptist Church of Boston**★ (Commonwealth Ave. at Clarendon St.) boasts a puddingstone facade and a 176-foot-tall tower.

The Best of Back Bay

Boston Public Library★★
700 Boylston St. on Copley Sq.
See Landmarks.

Christian Science Center★★
175 Huntington Ave. 617-450-2000. http://christianscience.com. Open year-round. Free tours Tue–Sat afternoons, Sun 11am. No tours major holidays.
This stunning ensemble of bold concrete structures, surrounding an enormous reflecting pool (670ft by 100ft), houses the world headquarters of the Christian Science church. The grand **Mother Church Extension** (1906) holds

A New Church

Mary Baker Eddy founded Christian Science in 1866. She credited reading a Gospel account of one of Jesus' healings with her quick recovery from a serious injury. The religion is based on her conviction that there is science behind Jesus' healings demonstrable today.

Extension, Christian Science Center

©Physicist.ed/Wikimedia Commons

Commonwealth Avenue

© Greater Boston CVB/FayFoto, Inc.

one of the 10-largest organs in the country, with more than 13,000 pipes. The Romanesque-style original church (1894), with its rough granite facade and bell tower, connects to the rear of the extension.

Named for the founder of Christian Science, a New Englander, the **Mary Baker Eddy Library for the Betterment of Humanity** opened in 2002. Step inside to experience the **Mapparium**, a 30-foot walk-through glass-paneled globe that represents the worldwide scope of the church's publishing activities. The library includes the Hall of Ideas, the Quest Gallery and The Monitor Gallery, with exhibits on *The Christian Science Monitor*, an international daily newspaper published by the church since 1908.

Commonwealth Avenue★★

It's easy to imagine yourself in late-19C Paris when you see this 200-foot-wide thoroughfare. "Comm Ave," as the locals call it, recalls the grand boulevards laid out during Napoleon III's reign; it remains a coveted address today. Lined with elm trees and punctuated with commemorative statues, this broad avenue's

pleasant mall makes a good place to view a sampling of Back Bay houses on either side. At the southwest corner of Commonwealth Avenue and Dartmouth Street, the sprawling **Vendome** (1871) was once Back Bay's most luxurious hotel; it served as a temporary home to such celebrities as Oscar Wilde, Mark Twain, Sarah Bernhardt and Ulysses S. Grant. In the 1970s it was transformed into condominiums.

Copley Square★★
Bounded by Boylston, Dartmouth, & Clarendon Sts.
Named for painter **John Singleton Copley** *(see box p 27)*,

---

Image Maker

Before the days of photographs, people had their portrait painted for posterity, if they could afford it. America's first important portraitist was **John Singleton Copley** (1738–1815). His paintings of well-known citizens of his day conveyed an amazingly accurate likeness of them. You can see his attention to detail in his portrait of Paul Revere in the Museum of Fine Arts, Boston *(see Museums)*.

this is Back Bay's main public square; it shows off some of Boston's most celebrated architectural treasures, like Trinity Church, the John Hancock Tower and the Public Library *(see Landmarks)*. Today it's hard to believe that the area was once a railroad yard.

John Hancock Tower★★
St. James Ave. See Landmarks.

Public Garden★★
Bounded by Arlington, Boylston, Charles & Beacon Sts. See Parks and Gardens.

Beacon Hill★★

The cozy, one-square-mile enclave, bordered by Beacon Street, Bowdoin Street, Cambridge Street and Storrow Drive, shows off cobblestone streets, brick walkways, gas lamps and well-maintained historic brownstones. Magnolia trees line narrow streets and window boxes overflow with flowers.

Historically the home of Boston Brahmins and the city's early black community, the Hill is the only remnant of the three peaks that made up Trimountain ridge, which once rose on the western side of the city. Its name stems from the primitive beacon that the Puritans raised on its summit in 1634 to warn of invasion by the Indians. From 1799 until the mid-19C, developers transformed the Trimountain area: Beacon Hill's summit was lowered 60 feet and the two neighboring peaks were leveled, the present street system was laid out, and the pretty enclave of English-style brick residences that we know as Beacon Hill came into being. The south slope, between Pinckney Street and the Common, became the bastion of Boston's affluent society *(see box below)*. The north slope became the center of Boston's black community in the 19C, many of whose members worked for the well-to-do on the Hill. Today, a stroll along Beacon Hill's serene streets will transport you to a bygone era.

Beacon Hill Breakdown
Bordering the Public Garden and Boston Common *(see Parks and Gardens)*, **Beacon Street★** is lined

Beacon Hill

© Gwen Cannon/Michelin

Past Residents
The "Hill" oozes Old World charm and old money. In fact, its residents, past and present, read like a Who's Who of politicians and authors: John and Abigail Adams, Daniel Webster, Henry David Thoreau, Ralph Waldo Emerson, John F. Kennedy, author Robin Cook and Secretary of State John Kerry are a few who have lived in this exclusive neighborhood.

with stately buildings, the most prominent among them being the golden-domed **State House**★★ (see Landmarks). The stone and brick facade of the **Bull and Finch Pub** (84 Beacon St.), popularized by the 1980s television series Cheers, draws TV fans for a glimpse (and maybe a pint). **Charles Street**★, Beacon Hill's commercial hub, teems with restaurants, antique shops, cafes, vegetable and fruit stands, and other neighborhood businesses.

It's worth setting aside a full day for Beacon Hill, to explore both the neighborhood's past and its vibrant present. To link the two, stay in **The Liberty Hotel**, partially housed in a 19C jail (see Must Stay). Then, spend the morning touring the cobblestone streets and the **Black Heritage Trail** (see History), followed by a move into the present with an afternoon of shopping Charles, a rejuvenating glass of wine at **Bin 26 Enoteca** (see Nightlife) and dinner at **The Beacon Hill Bistro** (see Must Eat).

Massachusetts State House★★
24 Beacon St. See Landmarks.

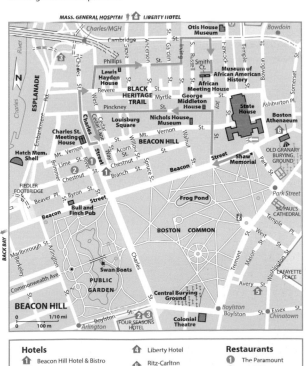

Hotels

1. Beacon Hill Hotel & Bistro
2. Four Seasons Hotel Boston
3. John Jeffries House
4. Liberty Hotel
5. Ritz-Carlton Boston Common
6. XV Beacon

Restaurants

1. The Paramount
2. 75 Chestnut
3. Bristol Lounge

Louisburg Square★★
Mt. Vernon St. at Willow St.
This tiny residential park is Boston's most prestigious address. Laid out in 1826 on pastureland purchased from John Singleton Copley, the square now boasts multimillion-dollar restored brownstones hugging brick walkways. The Vanderbilts once lived here; today, other well-heeled Bostonions call the area around the square home.

Boston Athenaeum★
10 1/2 Beacon St. 617-227-0270.
http://bostonathenaeum.org.
Open Mon–Wed 9am–8pm, Thu–Fri 9am–5:30pm, Sat 9am–4pm.
Closed major holidays.
Established in 1807, the Boston Athenaeum is one of the nation's oldest private lending libraries. It also features an art gallery and a children's library, a perfect place for families to take a break from their busy sightseeing schedule.

North End★★
North of N. Washington & Cross Sts. See map p 41.
Rooftop gardens; shops bulging with fresh meats, poultry and vegetables; and restaurants and cafes that serve home-cooked pasta, pizza, pastries and espresso crowd this colorful Italian district. Boston's oldest residential neighborhood has been continuously inhabited since 1630. Throughout the 17C and 18C, the North End reigned as Boston's principal residential district and included a community of free blacks. Irish and Jewish immigrants who settled here in the 19C eventually moved on, replaced by Southern Italian immigrants, who have maintained a strong presence.

Hanover Street★ and **Salem Street** are the main thoroughfares running through this compact, one-mile-square burg, crisscrossed by a network of narrow streets and alleyways. You can soak up the Old World atmosphere by meandering the streets, and poking into the tiny *salumerias* (delis), *pasticcerias* (pastry shops) and *macellerias* (meat markets). Finish your shopping at some of the boutiques that have moved into the neighborhood in recent years, including **in-jean-ius** (see

The Butcher, the Baker, the Pasta Maker

Get an insider's look at eating and shopping on a **North End Market Tour** led by Michele Topor. On the 3hr walk, you'll follow Topor to her favorite haunts; learn to select the best olive oil and pasta; and taste samples along the way. She also runs a Chinatown tour. *617-523-6032. www.bostonfoodtours.com. Tours year-round Wed & Sat 10am–1pm & 2pm–5pm, Fri 10am–1pm & 3pm–6pm; $54 per person; reservations required.*

© Michele Topor Tours

Shopping). Then it's back to the old ways: grab a seat at one of the sidewalk cafes for an espresso, and listen to the old-timers chat about their neighbors. Tourists flock over from Faneuil Hall, following the redbrick **Freedom Trail★★★** to Paul Revere's House and the North Church *(see Historic Sites)*. The local community in the North End continues to celebrate numerous saint's days throughout the year (schedules of feasts are posted in storefronts and churches). These lively events feature religious processions, outdoor entertainment and an abundance of food sold by street vendors.

Copp's Hill Burying Ground★
Next to Old North Church, bordered by Hull & Charter Sts. See Historic Sites.

🍴 **North End Eateries**
One of the favorite pastimes in Boston's North End? Eating! If you'd like to bring home a taste of Italy, visit **Maria's Pastry Shop** *(46 Cross St.; 617-523 1196; www. northendboston.com/marias)* or **Modern Pastry** *(257 Hanover St.; 617-523-3783; www.modernpastry.com)* for homemade cannoli and flaky sfogliatella; and **Salumeria Italiana** *(151 Richmond St.; 617-523-8743; www.salumeriaitaliana.com)* for imported pastas, artisanal balsamic vinegars and other Italian specialty foods. The Salumeria guys will happily ship your selections home so there's no need to worry about getting that big bottle of expensive olive oil you had home. Or, for a perfect picnic in a North End park *(see Parks & Gardens)*, buy some of the cured meats on display. Don't miss a stop at

Freshly baked bread in the North End
©Chee-Onn Leong/Bigstockphoto.com

V. Cirace & Son, Inc. *(173 North St., 617-227-3193; http://vcirace.com)*, a beautifully decked-out, third-generation wine store that's been in the North End since 1906. Here's a sampling of our favorite places for Italian fare:
Bricco – *241 Hanover St. 617-248-6800. www.bricco.com.* Upscale Bricco's modern Italian ristorante has been a local favorite for years. Try dishes like the wild boar and mushroom ragu or gnocchi baked with made-in-house mozzarella.
Giacomo's – *355 Hanover St. See Must Eat.*
Taranta – *210 Hanover St. 617-720-0052. www.tarantarist.com.* This small, upscale dining room serves up creative southern Italian fare with Peruvian influences. Try the appetizer of mini calzoni stuffed with three different fillings.
Regina Pizzeria – *11½ Thacher St. 617-227-0765. www. reginapizzeria.com.* In the mood for pizza? You can't go wrong at this tiny North End eatery, which has been serving its legendary thin-crust pizza for nearly 80 years.
If you're not in the mood to sit (or wait), most of the neighborhood bakeries serve up square slices for about $1.25 that are easy to eat on-the-go.

The Waterfront★

Along Atlantic Ave. See map p 41.
During Boston's long period of maritime prosperity, sailing ships brimming with exotic cargoes frequented the busy harbor. Today this area is home to the **New England Aquarium★★★** *(see Musts for Kids)*, a string of waterside promenades, upscale hotels, waterfront restaurants, and bustling wharves offering scenic harbor views. Constructed in the 1830s, the granite buildings on **Commercial Wharf** and **Lewis Wharf** were renovated in the 1960s into modern harborfront offices and luxury apartments. The original 1710 Long Wharf stretched like a monumental avenue from the Custom House Tower some 2,000 feet into the harbor to service large craft unable to anchor closer to the shore. Over the centuries its length was cut in half and its row of shops and warehouses demolished. The low-scale profile of the large, brick **Marriott Long Wharf Hotel** *(see Must Stay)* harmonizes well with the traditional architecture of the waterfront.

What's What along the Waterfront

New England Aquarium★★★
Central Wharf. See Musts for Kids.

Custom House Block
Long Wharf.
Occupying a fine site on the wharf's edge, the 1837 granite Custom House Block has been converted into a mixed-use commercial and residential complex. The 496-foot tower, a city landmark, was added to the custom house in 1915.

Long Wharf
At the end of State St., at Atlantic Ave.
The docking point for sightseeing cruises of the harbor, Long Wharf is also the departure dock for Boston's **water taxi** *(see p 15)* for the **Charlestown Navy Yard** *(see Historic Sites).*

Chinatown

See map inside front cover.
Bounded by Washington, Boylston & Kneeland Sts. and the John F. Fitzgerald Expwy.

Custom House at night

MUST SEE

Centered on Beach Street, Boston's historic Chinatown, the third oldest in America, is rather small compared to its counterparts in New York and San Francisco. But the tiny neighborhood, squeezed between South Station and the Boston Common, is crammed with ethnic restaurants, exotic shops and more than 6,000 residents. The prettiest—and most traditional-looking—entrance into the neighborhood is from **Chinatown Park** on the **Kennedy Greenway** *(see Parks & Gardens)*. Walk under the **Chinatown Gate** *(Beach & Surface Sts.)* into this colorful, dynamic (and slightly seedy) enclave, and you're instantly in a different world that, in look and vibe, has little to do with the rest of Boston. It's easy to walk around Chinatown; join the crowds and browse the unusual shops and markets. At **Nam Bac Hong Inc.** *(75 Harrison Ave.; 617-426-8227)*, you'll find a host of Chinese teas and herbal concoctions guaranteed to cure whatever ails you. Supermarkets, like the **Sun Sun Co.** *(18 Oxford St.; 617-426-6494)*, teem with people and exotic foods; the aisles and

Best Dim Sum

For the best dim sum in town, grab a table at the always crowded **China Pearl** *(9 Tyler St.; 617-426-4338)*, where the waitstaff pushes carts brimming with choices: Peking dumplings, barbecue pork, shrimp nuggets and more. Another popular place for dim sum is **Empire Garden Restaurant**, housed in a former 1940s movie theater *(690 Washington St.; 617-482-8898)*.

counters are filled with teas and herbs, strange veggies and roots, live fish and other sea creatures. If tightly-packed crowds don't bother you, the best time to visit Chinatown is during one of the annual street festivals. In summer, during the first three weeks of August, the **August Moon Festival** is celebrated; in late January or early February, **Chinese New Year** is ushered in. Both feature dragon parades, fireworks, martial-arts demonstrations, food and dancing. Otherwise, stick to the still-busy days and nights the rest of the year.

Chinatown Gate

公 為 下 天

肥牛火鍋城

Hot Pot B

NEIGHBORHOODS

Downtown

See map p41. North and east of Boston Common.

Stretching from Boston Common northeast to Haymarket, downtown embraces the city's historic heart, its commercial district and the seat of city government. The renovation of **Faneuil Hall Marketplace★★** *(see Shopping)* in the 1970s dramatically revived the ambience of downtown by injecting new vitality into the city's center. **Downtown Crossing** *(see Shopping)*, which was completed in the same time period, produced a similar effect; this outdoor walking mall is the focus of what is now a bustling retail district.

Faneuil Hall★★★
Dock Sq., main entrance facing Quincy Market. See Landmarks.

City Hall★★
Congress & State Sts., across from Faneuil Hall. 617-635-4500. www.cityofboston.gov. Open year-round Mon–Fri 8:30am–5:30pm. Closed major holidays.

Imagine being a city council member in Boston. You would come for council meetings to this top-heavy concrete structure with a brick base. One of Boston's controversial architectural statements since its completion in 1968, the building recalls the works of architect Le Corbusier and helped bring the so-called Brutalist style to prominence in the US. If you're architecturally minded, you'll enjoy exploring the vast public spaces on the lower floors. Oh, and you can watch a city council meeting from the fifth-floor galleries *(Wednesdays at noon)*.

Boston Common★★★
Bordered by Boylston, Tremont, Park & Beacon Sts. See Parks and Gardens.

Haymarket
Blackstone St. See Shopping.

Union Street
When you've exhausted your shopping and eating options at Faneuil Hall Marketplace, check out Union Street. During the late 18C, this street was lined with taverns and pubs. The Duke of Orleans, who later became King Louis-Philippe of France, lived for several months on the second floor of the venerable **Union Oyster House** *(see Must Eat)*, where he gave French lessons to earn his keep. Daniel Webster was also a frequent patron here.

While on Union Street, don't miss an opportunity to walk through the **New England Holocaust Memorial★** *(see Landmarks)*.

Charlestown★
See map on inside front cover.

Across Boston Harbor, you'll find one of the city's oldest historic areas, easily recognized by its prominent stone obelisk, the **Bunker Hill Monument** *(see Historic Sites)*. During the Battle of Bunker Hill in 1775, Charlestown's colonial dwellings were destroyed by the British and replaced following the Revolution by rows of Federal-style houses that line Main and Warren streets. The opening of the **Charlestown Navy Yard** *(see Historic Sites)* in 1800 made Charlestown a renowned shipbuilding center. The Freedom Trail takes in the major sights of Charlestown.

MUST SEE

The Fenway

See map on inside front cover.
West of Back Bay, this area is home to the Museum of Fine Arts, Isabella Stewart Gardner Museum, Fenway Park, and several institutions of higher education such as Boston University. The Fenway is also the name of a road that parallels the Emerald Necklace *(see Parks & Gardens)* and the Muddy River.

RISING STARS

Some Boston neighborhoods are long-time favorites of both visitors and locals; others have just recently started taking some of the spotlight for themselves. Two to watch—and, of course, visit:

South End★

See map p25.
South of Back Bay, the once-rundown, now urban-chic South End, bordered roughly by Massachusetts and Columbus avenues and Albany and East Berkeley streets (though the boundaries are a bit fuzzy), is one of Boston's most-talked-about neighborhoods. The gentrification of this Victorian corner, with its narrow, brownstone-lined streets, parks and fountains, began in the 1980s when gays and lesbians, and artists and musicians moved in. Today you'll find trendy restaurants, a lively night scene and restored town houses with million-dollar price tags. South End has attracted cultural institutions such as the **Boston Center for the Arts★★** *(539 Tremont St.; 617 426-5000; www.bcaonline.org)*, which resides in the landmark Cyclorama Building (1884). Home to artistic groups such as the SpeakEasy Stage Company and the Community

Music Center of Boston, the BCA offers Bostonians and visitors a full calendar of art exhibits, theater and musical and dance performances *(see Performing Arts)*.

Fort Point Channel★

Fort Point Channel has a way to go before it's a well-known neighborhood name around Boston. To many, Fort Point Channel is just the (not so beautiful) body of water that runs between the downtown business district and South Boston. Tell them it's the area around the **Boston Children's Museum** *(see Musts for Kids)* and they'll probably correct you with a *"nah, that's the Seaport district and convention center area."* Yes, but for more than 20 years, its artier residents have called it Fort Point Channel. Now that the big gun of the modern art scene, the **ICA** *(see Museums)* has taken up residence in the neighborhood, the name is slowly starting to gain traction. Whatever you call it, spend some time there. The museums are top-notch, the views of the harbor are incredible *(www.bostonharborwalk.com)*, the chowder at **Yankee Lobster** *(see Must Eats)* is thick with the best from Boston's waters and the almost-daily beer tastings at **Harpoon Brewery** *(306 Northern Ave.; 617-456-2322; www.harpoonbrewery.com; 1hr tours Mon–Wed noon–5pm, Thu–Fri noon–6pm; $5)* are a perfect capper on a Fort Point Channel afternoon. If you are in town the third weekend of October, go inside local artists' studios during the **Fort Point Arts Community Art Walk** *(www.fortpointarts.org)*. You can also use this opportunity to buy their work.

CAMBRIDGE★★

No visit to Boston is complete without spending some time in Cambridge, which sits right across the Charles River. This oh-so-literate municipality and academic research center is home to renowned Harvard University, Massachusetts Institute of Technology (MIT) and Radcliffe Institute for Advanced Study (formerly Radcliffe College).

Chosen as the Bay Colony's capital in 1630, Cambridge has its historic side. Stroll down **Brattle Street★**, where wealthy Tories (loyal to the British Crown) built homes in the 1700s. General George Washington used the house at no. 105 as his headquarters during the siege of Boston; between 1837 and 1882 poet Henry Wadsworth Longfellow lived in this house, where he penned *Evangeline* (1847) and *The Song of Hiawatha* (1855). Today the home pays homage to both men as the **Longfellow House - Washington's Headquarters National Historic Site★** *(617-876-4491; www.nps.gov/long; visit by 1hr guided tour only May–late Oct Wed–Sun hourly from 10am–4pm).*
To the east spreads **Cambridge Common** *(bounded by Garden St. & Massachusetts Ave.)*, the town center for more than 300 years. From 1775 to 1776, it was the site of General

Touring Tip

To get your bearings: Massachusetts Avenue ("Mass Ave" to locals) runs the length of Cambridge, extending from Harvard Bridge, past MIT and through Harvard Square. Memorial Drive borders the Charles River.

Washington's main camp. Off the Common's southwest corner sits **Christ Church** *(0 Garden St.; 617-876-0200; http://cccambridge.org)*, the oldest church in Cambridge, built in 1760. Today the always-bustling **Harvard Square** *(Massachusetts Ave. & John F. Kennedy St.; http://harvardsquare.com)*, two blocks south of the Common, serves as the city's hub.

Touring Tip

Haute couture isn't part of the dress code on the streets of Cambridge—almost everybody walks almost everywhere, so the only local requirements are comfortable shoes and a carry-it-all-with-you bag. The Harvard Square area teems with shops, clubs and eateries. Readers should go straight to the family-owned **Harvard Book Store** *(1256 Mass. Ave.; 617-661-1515; www.harvard.com)*. At the **Harvard Square Coop** *(1400 Mass. Ave.; 617-499-2000; www.thecoop.com)*, nearly everything has a Harvard or MIT logo on it. Nearby, **Club Passim** *(47 Palmer St.; 617-492-7679; http://clubpassim.org)* showcases big-name folk musicians. Don't miss **L.A. Burdick Chocolate Shop & Café** *(52 Brattle St.; 617-491-4340; www.burdickchocolate.com)*; their pastries and hot chocolate are pure delight!

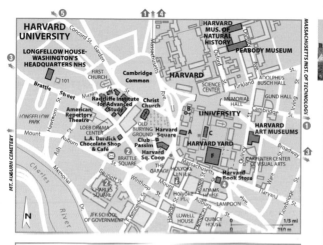

Hotels		Mary Prentiss Inn	3	Jasper White's
1 A Cambridge House		**Restaurants**	4	Mr. Bartley's Burger Cottage
2 Charles Hotel	1	East Coast Grill		Rialto 2
3 Hotel Marlowe	2	Harvest	5	T.W. Food

Harvard University★★★

Campus borders the Charles River off Memorial Dr. (west of MIT). 617-495-1000. www.harvard.edu. Red Line to Harvard T stop.

Harvard is old, really old. The first college established in America, it was founded in 1636 to train young men as leaders of church, state and trade. The school's first class had nine students and one master; enrollment has grown to some 21,000 degree candidates. In 1879 **Radcliffe College** (now Radcliffe Institute for Advanced Study) was founded to provide women with equal access to a Harvard education. Harvard's superior academic traditions, distinguished faculty and devotion to research have made it one of the world's leading institutions of higher learning. The school's endowment, which grew to almost $33 billion by 2013, is the largest of any university

in the world. It is shared by the undergraduate college and 10 graduate schools.

A city within a city, Harvard's campus has some 500 buildings, including more than 100 libraries, 9 museums and dozens of laboratories—and it's still growing. Only first-year students live in the famed dorms in and around Harvard Yard; yet, throughout their

Touring Tip

Pick up a campus map or join a student-led tour at the **Harvard Information Center**, located in the Smith Center Arcade *(1350 Mass. Ave.; 617-495-1573; open year-round Mon–Sat 9am–5pm)*. Tours (1hr) depart Mon–Sat 10am, noon & 2pm during the academic year; call for summer hours.

CAMBRIDGE

time at the school, most students do live on campus.

Though most people don't immediately think of athletics when the Harvard name is mentioned, Crimson fans are a dedicated lot (especially if their team is playing football or rowing against their long-standing archrival Yale).

What's What on Harvard's Campus?

Harvard Yard★★ – *Bounded by Mass Ave. & Peabody, Cambridge & Quincy Sts*. The oldest part of the university, Harvard Yard includes 1720 **Massachusetts Hall [A** *on map p37*], the oldest Harvard building still standing; **Holden Chapel [B** *on map p37*], the university's first official chapel; and **University Hall [C** *on map p 37*] (1815), fronted by Daniel Chester French's statue of college founder John Harvard.

Harvard Museum of Natural History★★ – *26 Oxford St. 617-495-3045. http://hmnh.harvard.edu. Open year-round daily 9am–5pm. Closed Jan 1, Thanksgiving Day &* *Dec 24-25. $12 adults, $8 children (ages 3-18), includes admission to the adjacent Peabody Museum.* Created in 1998, this illustrious museum holds some 12,000 specimens and artifacts that make up Harvard's outstanding research collections. The highlight is the Ware Collection of nearly 4,000 **Blaschka Glass Flowers**★★★. Crafted in Germany by Leopold and Rudolph Blaschka between 1887 and 1936, the hand-crafted glass models accurately represent 847 species of flowering plants. The pieces were created as a teaching tool, but they've clearly crossed over into art. Another highlight is the newly renovated **Earth and Planetary Sciences gallery**, where 3,000 numerous minerals, gemstones and meteorites are displayed; don't miss the eye-catching giant gypsum crystals from Mexico. Head through the **New England Forests** exhibit to find huge whales in the two-story **Great Mammal Hall**, which underwent a 2009 overhaul to make it look as if it were new in 1872.

Harvard Museum of Natural History

MUST SEE

Peabody Museum of Archaeology & Ethnology★ –

11 Divinity Ave. 617-496-1027. https://peabody.harvard.edu. Same hours as Museum of Natural History, above.
Founded in 1866, the Peabody Museum is among the oldest archaeological and ethnographic museums in the world, with one of the finest collections of human cultural history found anywhere. Its three floors of exhibits range from towering Native American totem poles and large Maya sculptures to precious artifacts of the ancient world. Be sure to see the exhibit on colonial Harvard and its Indian College, and the new exhibit, The Legacy of Penobscot Canoes: A View from the River.

Harvard Art Museums★ –

32 Quincy St. 617-495-9400. www.harvardartmuseums.org. Currently closed until completion of new facility, opening fall 2014.
Harvard's longstanding art institutions, the **Fogg Museum**, **Busch-Reisinger Museum** and **Arthur M. Sackler Museum**, unite in a new facility designed by acclaimed Italian architect Renzo Piano, to open in fall 2014. The central courtyard on the ground floor, topped with a glass roof, will definitely impress viewers. Surrounding galleries on the first, second, and third floors showcase artworks in all media, from ancient times to the present. Strengths of the collections include Italian early Renaissance paintings, Impressionist and post-Impressionist works, German Expressionism and materials from the Bauhaus, archaic Chinese jades and bronzes, Greek vases and Mediterranean coins, and works on paper from Islamic lands and India.

Massachusetts Institute of Technology★

The campus borders the Charles River along Memorial Dr. & Massachusetts Ave. 617-253-4795. www.mit.edu. Red Line to Kendall/MIT T stop.

One of the nation's premier science and research universities, the Massachusetts Institute of Technology (MIT) is a world leader in research and development, with schools of Engineering, Science, Architecture and Planning, Management, and Humanities and Social Science. Some 11,000 students from 50 states and 117 foreign countries are enrolled here.

MIT Museum★ – *265 Massachusetts Ave., Building N51. 617-253-5927. http://web.mit.edu/museum. Open year-round daily 10am–5pm. Closed major holidays. $10.* A gadget-lover's delight, this fun house of mind-boggling innovation includes stop-motion photographs, kinetic sculptures, robots and the world's largest collection of holograms. Exhibits that will definitely inspire and amaze are **5,000 Moving Parts**, and **Robots and Beyond**. In the **Hart Nautical Gallery** *(55 Massachusetts Ave., Building 5)*, models illustrate 1000 years of ship building.

List Visual Arts Center – *20 Ames St., Building E-15. 617-253-4680. http://listart.mit.edu. Hours change depending on the show and season. Call for updated details.* There's life beyond science at MIT; see the school's collection of contemporary art as well as the always-interesting temporary exhibits, in this building designed by MIT grad, the renowned I.M. Pei.

CAMBRIDGE

HISTORIC SITES

Few places in the country can rival Boston's historical past. Boston is, after all, the place where the American Revolution began. It's the site of the Boston Tea Party and the Boston Massacre. Patriots Paul Revere, John Hancock, James Otis and Samuel Adams made history here and were later buried here. There's no escaping the past in Beantown—it's pretty much everywhere (and Bostonians wouldn't have it any other way)!

National Park Service

Old Granary Burying Ground

The Freedom Trail★★★

See map, opposite. The Freedom Trail begins at the Greater Boston Convention & Visitor Center, 148 Tremont St. on Boston Common. 888-733-2678. www.thefreedom trail.org. Visitor center open year-round Mon–Sat 8:30am–5pm, Sun 9am–5pm; closed Thanksgiving Day & Dec 25. Take the MBTA Green Line or Red Line to the Park Street T stop.

Just follow the red brick (or painted) road (ok, line) to Boston's most historic sites and attractions. The trail, which celebrated its 50th birthday in 2008, is a 2.5-mile line that weaves through Boston's

Actions Leading to the Revolutionary War

1765 – The English Parliament passes the Stamp Act and the Quartering Act, requiring colonists to house British troops. The Sons of Liberty, an underground organization, forms in many of the colonies.

1767 – The English Parliament passes the Townshend Revenue Acts, imposing a new series of taxes on the colonists.

1768 – Samuel Adams urges the colonists to unite against the British government and fight taxation without representation.

1770 – The Boston Massacre occurs on March 5.

1773 – On December 16, Patriots stage the Boston Tea Party.

1775 – On April 18, Paul Revere rides to warn against the advancing Redco

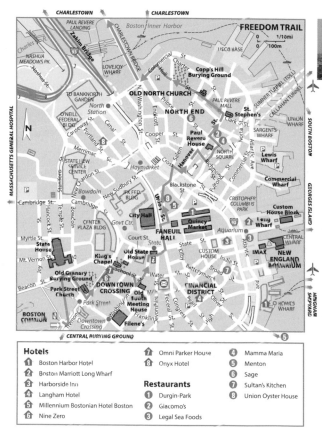

CHARLESTOWN   CHARLESTOWN

PAUL REVERE LANDING

Boston Inner Harbor

0   1/10mi
0   100m

USCG BASE

Zakim Bridge

Charles

NASHUA MEADOWS PK.

LOVEJOY WHARF

SUMMER TUNNEL (TOLL)

CALLAHAN TUNNEL

SOUTH BOSTON

CHARLESTOWN BRIDGE

Commercial St   Charter St

Copp's Hill Burying Ground

TO BANKNORTH GARDEN

North Station

O'NEILL FEDERAL BLDG

Washington St

Prince St

Endicott St

OLD NORTH CHURCH

PAUL REVERE MALL

St. Stephen's

SARGENTS WHARF

UNION WHARF

Canal St

Portland St

Cooper St

NORTH END

Clark St

Salem St

Causeway St

N

MASSACHUSETTS GENERAL HOSPITAL

Merrimac St

STATE VIEW SERVICE CENTER

Chardon St

Haymarket

Hanover St

Paul Revere House

NORTH SQUARE

Richmond St

Fulton St

Atlantic Ave

Commercial St

Lewis Wharf

Commercial Wharf

GEORGES ISLAND

Cross St

Blackstone St

CRISTOPHER COLUMBUS PARK

Custom House Block

Cambridge St

New Sudbury St

JFK FED BLDG

Union St

Bowdoin St

Cambridge St

CENTER PLAZA BLDG

City Hall

Govt Ctr.

Quincy Market

FANEUIL HALL

Long Wharf

Aquarium

CENTRAL WHARF

Myrtle St

State House

Temple St

Hancock St

Beacon St

Court St

King's Chapel

Old State House

State St

CUSTOM HOUSE

India St

IMAX

NEW ENGLAND AQUARIUM

Mt. Vernon St

School St

Water St

Kilby St

Battery march St

Broad St

HINGHAM SHIPYARD

Old Granary Burying Ground

Park Street Church

DOWNTOWN CROSSING

Old South Meeting House

Milk St

FINANCIAL DISTRICT

Oliver St

ROWE'S WHARF

Park Street

BOSTON COMMON

Filene's

Congress St

Federal St

Franklin St

Downtown Crossing

CENTRAL BURYING GROUND

Hotels

1. Boston Harbor Hotel
2. Boston Marriott Long Wharf
3. Harborside Inn
4. Langham Hotel
5. Millennium Bostonian Hotel Boston
6. Nine Zero
7. Omni Parker House
8. Onyx Hotel

Restaurants

1. Durgin-Park
2. Giacomo's
3. Legal Sea Foods
4. Mamma Maria
5. Menton
6. Sage
7. Sultan's Kitchen
8. Union Oyster House

downtown streets, linking 16 historic sites. While you can just walk the whole thing straight (or, as the line dictates), it's also a great way to explore the neighborhoods it passes through. As you'll see, modern-day Boston and the city's historic sites are close neighbors. After grabbing a bite to eat or picking up a Red Sox t-shirt at a nearby shop, just return to the line when you're ready to step back in time. And don't feel you have to walk the entire trail in one day, unless you're pressed for time.

Sites Along the Trail

The following selected sites on the Freedom Trail are organized in the order they appear on the trail, which begins at Boston Common and leads through downtown, the North End, and over the Charlestown Bridge to Charlestown.

Boston Common★

Bordered by Boylston, Tremont, Park & Beacon Sts. *See Parks and Gardens.*

Looking out on the Common with an eye to history will put a

different spin on your next Frisbee® game in the park. The militia used the 44-acre Common as their training grounds and the British Army called it home during their occupation of the city.

State House★★
24 Beacon St., at the corner of Park St. See Landmarks.

Park Street Church★
Park & Tremont Sts. 617-523-3383. www.parkstreet.org. Open Jul–Aug Tue–Sat 9:30am–3:30pm. Closed Jul 4.
Step inside this 1809 meetinghouse to see the place where William Lloyd Garrison delivered his first antislavery speech (1829), and Samuel Francis Smith's "America" was sung for the first time (1831). Don't hurt your neck when you look up to take in the steeple: it's 217-feet high.

Old Granary Burying Ground★
Tremont St. 617-357-8300. Open year-round daily 9am–5pm.
Buried here are Samuel Adams, Paul Revere, John Hancock and the five colonists killed during the Boston Massacre. Why the Granary?

Touring Tip

To the rear of the State House, note the circle of cobblestones embedded in the traffic island in the busy intersection of Congress and State streets. It marks the actual Boston Massacre site. Five colonists were killed in this infamous clash between the Patriots and Redcoats on March 5, 1770.

Touring Tip

Don comfortable shoes, and plan on a half day or more to walk the entire trail. You can duck into several historic sites along the way. But there are also opportunities to shop, eat and rest. Short on time or energy? Step off the trail before it leaves the North End, heading for Charlestown. Or board a water taxi from Long Wharf to the Charlestown Navy Yard to visit the USS *Constitution (see Musts for Kids)*. On the fast track, head straight to the North End and Copp's Hill Burial Ground. From there, it's a brief walk to the Old North Church and the Paul Revere House. Or start at the Park Street T entrance at Boston Common, cross the street to Park Street Church and its Old Granary Burying Ground *(see below)*. Then head straight to Faneuil Hall.

It's named for the grain storage building that once stood on the site of the Park Street Church.

King's Chapel★
Corner of Tremont & School Sts. 617-227-2155. www.kings-chapel. org. Tours late May–early Sept Mon–Sat 10am–4pm, Sun 1:30pm–4pm.
Believe it or not, this 1754 granite building replaced the original wooden chapel built on the site in the 1680s. Nine years after the British evacuated Boston, this church, New England's first Anglican house of worship, was reborn as the first Unitarian church in America. Go inside to admire the striking interior, considered the

finest example of Georgian church architecture in North America. The adjoining **King's Chapel Burying Ground**★ *(617-357-8300; www.cityofboston.gov/freedomtrail; open year-round daily 9am–5pm)* is Boston's oldest cemetery, founded in 1630. This is the final resting place of John Winthrop (the Massachusetts Bay Colony's first governor), John Alden (son of Priscilla and John), and William Dawes, Paul Revere's riding mate, whom Longfellow doomed to obscurity by leaving him out of his famous poem, "The Midnight Ride of Paul Revere." While exploring the burial ground, note the wide range of headstones and epitaphs. Don't leave without getting a photo of Joseph Tapping's headstone; the skull-and-crossbones design is striking.

Old Corner Bookstore

[A] *(refers to map p 41) 3 School St., at the corner of Washington St. 617-442-1859. www.historicboston.org. Open year-round daily.*
This restored 18C building has long figured in Boston's publishing world. Between 1845 and 1865, the building housed the publisher Ticknor and Fields, who published the works of such New England literati as Harriet Beecher Stowe, Henry Wadsworth Longfellow and Ralph Waldo Emerson. Though the building has been on the site since 1718, it's actually not the original; the first one burned down during the Great Fire of 1711.
Though it is on the Freedom Trail, it is currently leased to a fast-food establishment.

Old South Meeting House★★

310 Washington St., at Milk St. 617-482-6439. www.oldsouthmeetinghouse.org. Open Apr–Oct daily 9:30am–5pm. Nov–Mar daily 10am–4pm. Closed major holidays. $6.

Old South Meeting House

©Ted Holt/Bigstockphoto.com

Noted orators Samuel Adams and James Otis led many of the protest meetings held at Old South prior to the Revolution. The momentous rally that took place on the evening of December 16, 1773, gave rise to the Boston Tea Party. Talking gave way to action as Samuel Adams exclaimed: "This

Old State House

© Greater Boston CVB/FayFoto, Inc.

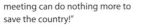

meeting can do nothing more to save the country!"

The story of the structure's history is told through interpretive displays and artifacts. It comes to life thanks to the "If These Walls Could Speak" audio exhibit that lets you listen in on recordings of passionate speeches and private conversations at various points throughout the interior.

Old State House★★

206 Washington St., at State St. 617-720-1713. www.bostonhistory.org. Open year-round daily 9am–5pm (Jun–Aug until 6pm). Closed Jan 1, first week February, Thanksgiving Day & Dec 25. $8.50.

This Georgian structure, Boston's oldest public building (1713), was the British government headquarters in the colonies until the Revolution. Though its cupola may be dwarfed by the city's modern skyscrapers, at one time it was the tallest building in Boston. In 1770 the Boston Massacre erupted on this site. On July 4, 1776, the colonies declared their independence in Philadelphia. Two weeks later, the Declaration of Independence was read from the balcony here, inciting the crowds to topple the lion and unicorn—symbols of the British Crown—perched on the structure's gables. (Shutterbugs take note: the restored lion and unicorn are waiting for you.) The Massachusetts government met here until the new State House was completed in 1798.

Inside, two floors feature excellent exhibits on the city, past and present. The historic balcony can be seen from the Council Chamber. The building also serves as the Bostonian Society's museum.

Faneuil Hall★★★

Dock Square, main entrance facing Quincy Market.
See Landmarks.

North End Pit Stops

By the time you reach North End on the Freedom Trail, you'll need a rest. Join the regulars for cioccalatto caldo and a cannoli at one of Hanover Street's Italian cafes. Try **Caffé Vittoria** (*290-296 Hanover St.; 617-227-7606; www.vittoriacaffe.com*), one of the oldest in the North End, or **Caffé Paradiso** (*255 Hanover St.; 617-742-1768; www.caffeparadiso.com*).

Paul Revere House★
19 North Square, North End.
See Landmarks.

Old North Church★★★
193 Salem St., North End.
See Landmarks.

Copp's Hill Burying Ground★
*Next to Old North Church, bordered
by Hull & Charter Sts. 617-635-4505.
Open year-round daily 9am–5pm.*
In the North End, next to Old North
Church, Copp's Hill rises high above
Charter Street, offering great views
across the water to Charlestown.
The cemetery's residents include
three generations of the prominent
Mather family: Increase (minister
and Harvard president), Cotton
(clergyman and writer), and his
son Samuel. The Mather plots are
located in the northeast corner
of the cemetery near the Charter
Street gate. Also interred here are
African-American abolitionist and
Revolutionary soldier Prince Hall,
and hundreds of black Bostonians
who settled in the North End in the
18C. Note the bullet holes made
by British riflemen, who used the
gravestones for target practice.
*The Freedom Trail continues across
Boston Harbor in* **Charlestown★**
(see map on inside front cover).

USS Constitution★★
Chelsea St., Charlestown Navy Yard.
See Musts for Kids.

Bunker Hill Monument
*Monument Square, Charlestown.
Open year-round daily 9am–
4:30pm (Jul–Aug until 5:30pm).*
Built in 1842, this soaring 221-foot-
tall granite obelisk marks the
spot of the infamous Battle of
Bunker Hill, the first major battle

Touring Tip

Don't miss the **Battle of
Bunker Hill Museum**, across
from the Monument *(617-212-
5601; www.nps.gov/bost; open
year-round daily 9am–5pm;
closed Jan 1, Thanksgiving Day
& Dec 25).* It's free, and you'll
learn about the battle, the
building of the monument and
Charlestown.

of the American Revolution. You
may know the famous quote
associated with the battle. Colonel
William Prescott (or, at least,
that's who most historians credit)
directed colonists waiting to fight
advancing British troops, "Don't
fire until you see the whites of
their eyes!" Along with the history
lesson, enjoy views of Charlestown,
Boston and the harbor from the top
of the observatory, 294 steps up.

Black Heritage Trail★★
*See map p 29. Boston African
American National Historic Site,
15 State St., 9th Floor. 617-*

Bunker Hill Monument
©PhotoDisc

HISTORIC SITES

45

742-5415. www.nps.gov/boaf. Self-guided walking tour maps are available at the Museum of African American History, Boston at 46 Joy St.

African slaves were first brought to Boston in 1638, just eight years after the city's founding. There were more than 400 slaves in the city by 1705 and in the North End, Boston's first free black community had formed. By the end of the Revolution, the city's black population included more free blacks than slaves. The largest communities of free blacks in the 18C and 19C resided on West Street, between Pinckney and Cambridge streets, and on the North Slope of Beacon Hill. About 30 years ago, Boston's Black Heritage Trail was established. The trail winds 1.6 miles through the North Slope section of Beacon Hill and highlights 14 pre-Civil War structures. Please note: many of the buildings on the trail are now private residences. Capture the exteriors on camera but, unless it's clear that it's a public building, please don't knock.

The trail begins at the **Robert Gould Shaw Memorial**★ facing the State House. This memorial honors the leader and members of the 54th Massachusetts Regiment in the Civil War *(see sidebar, below)*. Here are some other highlights along the trail:

George Middleton House – *5–7 Pinckney St.* Built in 1797, this two-family house is the oldest standing wooden structure in Beacon Hill. Middleton was an early leader of the African-American community on Beacon Hill and a colonel of a black militia group called the Bucks of America, who fought in the Revolutionary War.

John J. Smith House – *86 Pinckney St.* Smith and his wife, Georgiana, were vocal leaders in the fight for equal school rights for black children in Boston. They lived in this brick home from 1878–1893. A barber who counted abolitionist and senator Charles Sumner as a friend and client, Smith later became the third African American member of the Massachusetts House of Representatives.

Charles Street Meeting House – *Charles & Mt. Vernon Sts.* Abolitionists William Lloyd Garrison

Shaw Memorial

The Shaw Civil War Monument on Beacon Street honors Col. Robert Gould Shaw and the 54th Massachusetts Regiment, the Union's first regiment of free black volunteers. Shaw was killed in 1863 during the Union assault on Fort Wagner in South Carolina. The handsome bronze relief is the work of 19C sculptor Augustus Saint-Gaudens.

MUST SEE

and Sojourner Truth spoke at this meeting house (c.1807). It later became an African Methodist Episcopal church, and now houses offices and shops.

Lewis Hayden House – *66 Phillips St.* The residence is named for its abolitionist owner, who was a former fugitive slave. Hayden once threatened to blow the house up if anyone came looking for runaway slaves; he had two kegs of gunpowder in the basement to back up his words.

Museum of African American History, Boston★ – *46 Joy St. 617-725-0022. www.afroammuseum.org. Open year-round Mon–Sat 10am–4pm. Closed Jan 1, Thanksgiving Day & Dec 25. $5.* Housed in the former Abiel Smith School, the country's first publicly funded school for black children, the Museum of African American History features changing exhibits on African Americans in colonial New England. A past exhibit featured the history of black entrepreneurs of the 18C and 19C. Don't miss the museum's gift shop, which offers an extensive selection of books about African-American history and culture. The museum also hosts lectures and other events throughout the year.

African Meeting House★ – *8 Smith Court. 617-720-2991. www.afroammuseum.org. Same hours as above museum.* This handsome brick edifice is the oldest standing African-American church in the US. Built in 1806 by black Baptists for worship services, it also functioned as a forum for supporters of the antislavery movement.

Before the Abiel Smith School was built, the African Meeting House was also used as a school, a role it regained in 1849 when, in protest against segregated education, many black Bostonians took their children out of the public school. The building is a National Historic Landmark.

Historic Days

Boston is a city of history, and Bostonians like to celebrate the city's role in American history in a big way. Here, some holidays worth building a visit around:

Patriots' Day

Though the shot heard round the world that kicked off the Revolutionary War was fired on April 19, the annual celebration of the event takes place on the third Monday of April. Sports fans look forward to the day off from work so they can watch a Red Sox game or the Boston Marathon *(www.bostonmarathon.org).* Other Bostonians, especially those with kids, stick to celebrating the history at events within the city or out at **Minute Man National Historical Park★** *(see Concord and Lexington in Excursions),* where there are parades and reenactments.

Independence Day

Celebrating America's independence is pretty much mandatory if you're in Boston on July 4th. After all, it's the place where it all began.

The holiday is also the unofficial start of summer in America. The best-known Independence Day outing is the Boston Pops' performance at the Hatch Shell on the Esplanade *(see Musts for Fun).* Don't miss the **reenactment of the reading of the Declaration of Independence** just as the colonists did in 1776- - read from the balcony of the Old State House to the crowds below.

LANDMARKS

Perhaps the most iconic image of Boston is the ornate and massive Trinity Church, reflected in the mirrored glass of its sleek neighbor, the 60-story John Hancock Tower. This odd couple symbolizes the marriage of the old and new that is Boston itself. Sure, the city boasts the oldest this, that, and the other thing, but Boston's landmarks are far from stuffy. From the steeple of the Old North Church to the golden dome of the State House, these scattered gems reflect what visitors—and residents—love most about Beantown.

Faneuil Hall★★★

Dock Sq., main entrance facing Quincy Market. 617-242-5642. www.nps.gov/bost. Open year-round daily 9am–5pm. Closed Jan 1, Thanksgiving Day & Dec 25. State T stop.

This hall was Boston's center of action during the years leading up to the Revolution. The revered landmark, nicknamed "the Cradle of Liberty," served as the town meeting hall, where the likes of orator Samuel Adams fired up colonists with protests against British taxes. Other noted American leaders who have addressed audiences here over the years include Susan B. Anthony, John

Touring Tip

Look atop Faneuil Hall's cupola to see the grasshopper weather vane commissioned by Peter Faneuil in 1742. Modeled after the gilded bronze weather vanes that crown the Royal Exchange in London, the grasshopper has symbolized the Port of Boston since the 18C. It had special significance to Sir Thomas Gresham, who laid the first stone of the Royal Exchange. Abandoned in a field as a child, he found his way out by following the sounds of grasshoppers.

F. Kennedy and Dr. Martin Luther King, Jr. Wealthy merchant Peter Faneuil (pronounced FAN-yul) presented the building to Boston way back in 1742, but it had to be rebuilt 20 years later, after a fire caused extensive damage.

The ground floor was designed to house a marketplace like one of Olde England's country markets. Follow the staircase up to see the large meeting hall on the second floor; the big painting that dominates the front wall is George P.A. Healy's *Daniel Webster's Second Reply to Hayne*.

On the third floor you'll find historical arms, uniforms, flags and

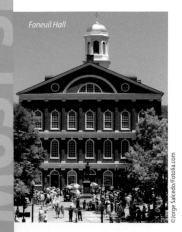

Faneuil Hall

©Jorge Salcedo/Fotolia.com

more in the museum of America's oldest military organization, the **Ancient and Honorable Artillery Company** *(617-227-1638; www.ahac.us.com; open year-round Mon–Fri 9am–3pm; closed major holidays).*

Old North Church★★★

193 Salem St. 617-523-6676. www.oldnorth.com. Open Jan–Feb daily 10am–4pm, Mar–May daily 9am–5pm, Jun–Oct daily 9am–6pm, Nov–Dec daily 9am–5pm. Closed Thanksgiving Day & Dec 25 (except for services). $3 contribution requested. Behind-the-scenes 30min tours $5. Haymarket T stop

The phrase "one if by land; two if by sea" might spring to mind when you visit this famous Boston landmark, also known now as Christ Church. It was here on the evening of April 18, 1775—you'll recall from your childhood history lessons—that the church sexton hung two lanterns in the steeple to signal that the British had departed Boston by boat on their way to Lexington and Concord. A century later, American poet Henry Wadsworth Longfellow immortalized this church in his poem "Paul Revere's Ride." An interesting fact: Revere's first connection to the church actually came years earlier. As a boy, he was a member of a bell-ringer's guild

Touring Tip

Step inside the combination gift shop and museum that's adjacent to Old North Church. You might just want to purchase a replica of the famed signal lantern as a memento of your Boston trip. Or how about a pewter candle snuffer like those used in colonial times? Historic flags, books and even tea are also for sale.

Old North Church

National Park Service

and was paid to ring the church bells each week.

The Old North Church was built in 1723; its tall spire was twice

North Church Bells

Walk around the North End on a Sunday morning and you'll be treated to the ringing of the bells at Old North Church. The eight change-ringing bells, cast by Abell Rudhall in Gloucester, England in 1744, are the oldest bells in North America. The bells were restored in 1975 for the Boston Bicentennial celebration and have been rung regularly ever since. Today, they summon an active Episcopal congregation to services.

LANDMARKS

49

replaced, and is now a hallowed city icon of the city. Inside the gleaming white **interior** are handsome boxed pews, an organ, an antique clock, and the pulpit where President Gerald Ford initiated the celebration of the nation's bicentennial in 1976. The four wooden cherubim located near the organ were part of the bounty captured from a French ship.

Museum of Fine Arts ★★★
465 Huntington Ave. See Museums.

Isabella Stewart Gardner Museum★★★
280 The Fenway. See Museums.

Boston Public Garden★★
Arlington & Charles Sts., Arlington T stop. See Parks and Gardens.

Boston Public Library★★
700 Boylston St., on Copley Square. 617-536-5400. www.bpl.org. Open year-round Mon–Thu 9am–9pm, Fri–Sat 9am–5pm, Sun 1pm–5pm. Closed major holidays. Copley T stop.

Founded in 1848, the Boston Public Library (BPL) was the first in the country to lend books. Today, it's still educating the city's younger generations, helping Bostonians satisfy their curiosity and get their hands on the latest bestseller.

The library also provides free Internet access, answers millions of questions, and serves up food in its on-site cafes, among other things. The stately Renaissance Revival-style building became the BPL's new home in 1895. It houses the

Courtyard, Boston Public Library

©Chee-Onn Leong/Fotolia.com

MUST SEE

Central Library; it, plus some 24 branches, compose the BPL. Before you enter, admire the granite facade's wrought-iron lanterns, relief panels by sculptor Augustus Saint-Gaudens and bronze doors by sculptor Daniel Chester French. The inside is even more elaborate, with such features as a staircase faced in Siena marble and mural paintings by French artist Puvis de Chavannes.

Courtyard (*Accessible from ground floor*) – Pause on the landing for a peek at the peaceful courtyard, a popular lunch spot for Bostonians.

Bates Hall (*2nd floor*) – You'll know you're in the halls of learning when you enter this vast reading room. The barrel vaulted ceiling is 50 feet high, and the long oak tables are topped with green-glass and brass lamps.

Upper Level Murals – Here you can wander through the cavernous rooms on the upper floors to admire murals by Edwin Abbey (*Quest of the Holy Grail; delivery room, 2nd floor*) and John Singer Sargent (*Judaism and Christianity; 3rd-floor corridor*). The library's extensive Joan of Arc collection is housed in the Cheverus Room (*3rd floor*).

Fenway Park★★
4 Yawkey Way.
See Musts for Fun.

Before Fenway
Boston and Fenway go together like, well, hotdogs and buns. But the stadium hasn't always been there. Before 1912, the Red Sox played their home games at the Huntington Avenue Grounds.

John Hancock Tower★★
Enter on St. James Ave.
Copley T stop.

It's a shame that the observation tower of this 62-story skyscraper is no longer open to the public. Until 2001 it was—and it provided a fine panorama of the city. (*You can still get a sky-high view from the 52nd floor of the Prudential; see Shopping.*) Since its completion in 1975, the I.M. Pei and Henry Cobb-designed Hancock Tower has reigned as New England's tallest skyscraper. Its unusual rhomboid shape creates a variety of profiles, depending on your vantage point. From the opposite side of Boylston Street, the tower, covered in 10,344 pieces of tempered glass, appears one-dimensional.

From other angles it's a gigantic mirror reflecting the sky and its neighbors, Trinity Church (*see p 53*) and the old John Hancock Building (1947), identifiable by its pyramid-shaped summit topped with a weather beacon.

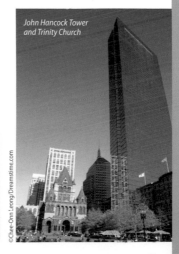

John Hancock Tower and Trinity Church

©Chee-Onn Leong/Dreamstime.com

LANDMARKS

State House

State House★★

24 Beacon St., at the corner of Park St. 617-727-3676. Tours year-round Mon–Fri 10am–3:30pm. Closed major holidays. Park St. T stop.

You can't help saying "oooh" when you first spot the golden dome of the state capitol building. The dome makes it so, well, stately. Completed in 1798 by prominent Boston architect Charles Bulfinch, the Massachusetts State House has been a cherished Beacon Hill landmark for more than two centuries. Check out the statues on the front lawn; they depict former Bostonians Anne Hutchinson, banished from the 17C colony for her religious views; Mary Dyer, hanged for her Quaker beliefs;

orator Daniel Webster; and Horace Mann, a pioneer in American education.

Doric Hall – The main entrance of the building leads into this hall, named for its rows of Doric columns. Step into **Nurses Hall** to view paintings that immortalize such events as Paul Revere's ride and the Boston Tea Party. The **Hall of Flags**, lined with paintings depicting scenes from early US history, was built to house the state collection of some 400 flags, including those from the Civil War and the Vietnam War.

Third Floor Hall – Take the main staircase to the third floor hall, where you'll find Daniel Chester French's statue of Roger Wolcott,

The Sacred Cod

Peek into the House of Representatives' chamber in the State House and you'll see a strange sight. No, we're not talking about the politicians! It's the life-size wooden carving of a codfish that hangs from the ceiling. (According to city legend, the cod always points toward the ruling party.) The carving was installed in the Old State House in 1784—a gift from a wealthy merchant—and later moved to its present location to acknowledge the importance of the cod industry to the Commonwealth. In 1933 pranksters from the Harvard Lampoon "codnapped" the fish. Chamber business stopped until it was recovered, several days later.

MUST SEE

governor of Massachusetts during the Spanish-American War. This floor contains the Governor's Office, as well as the Senate and House chambers and the Senate Reception Room.

Trinity Church★★

206 Clarendon St. 617-536-0944. http://trinitychurchboston. org. Open year-round Mon–Fri 11am–4:30pm, Sat 9am–4pm, Sun 1pm–5:30pm. Copley T stop.

Completed in 1877, this imposing granite and sandstone church was responsible for popularizing an architectural style in America now known as Richardsonian Romanesque. Trinity Church is considered the masterpiece of Henry H. Richardson. The American architect studied at the École des Beaux-Arts in Paris, where he was impressed by the power and richness of Romanesque architecture. So he took this style and added personal touches to it, such as short columns and solid quoins (decorative corner blocks) on his buildings' exteriors. The massive central tower of Trinity is similar to one of the towers of the Old Cathedral in Salamanca, Spain.

Step inside to see lavishly painted walls and murals and intricately carved religious scenes.

Paul Revere House★

19 North Square. 617-523-2338. www.paulreverehouse. org. Open mid-Apr–Oct daily 9:30am–5:15pm. Nov–mid-Apr daily 9:30am–4:15pm. Closed Jan 1, Thanksgiving Day & Dec 25 (and Mon Jan–Mar). $3. Haymarket T stop.

Look closely, especially if it's raining on the day you visit. The two-and-a-half-story wooden clapboard house is sometimes difficult to spot, since it's dwarfed by the taller buildings around it. Boston's oldest structure was built in 1680—it was already 90 years old when silversmith Paul Revere bought it in 1770. Revere started out on his historic ride to Lexington on April 18, 1775 from this dwelling. Inside, you'll see an account of the famous ride in Revere's own words, and Revere family furnishings, including silverware fashioned by Revere himself. Outside in the courtyard, you'll be amazed at the 900-pound bell made by Paul Revere and Sons

Paul Revere House

LANDMARKS

for the **USS Constitution**★★
(see Musts for Kids).
A new visitor center in a restored
building behind the Revere House
is slated to open in late 2014.

Symphony Hall★
301 Massachusetts Ave.
See Performing Arts.
Though it's an impressive job all on
its own, Symphony Hall isn't just
a home for the Boston Symphony
Orchestra and the Boston Pops. The
building (1900), which is renowned
for its incredible acoustics, houses
many treasures, including one
of the world's finest organs—an
Aeolian Skinner that was installed
60 years ago—and 16 replicas of
Greek and Roman statues that
celebrate music, art and literature.

Prudential Center★
800 Boylston St. 617-236-3100.
www.prudentialcenter.com.
Built in 1965, the 3.2 million
square foot Prudential Center
houses an astonishing number
of businesses—including offices,
retail spaces *(see Shopping)*
and restaurants, Boston's only
observatory, a post office and
many more. At 52 stories, it was
Boston's tallest skyscraper for the
first decade of its existence, until
upstaged in 1975 by the John
Hancock Tower, which rises eight
stories higher.

Chinatown Gate
Beach St. & Surface Rd.
Though the Chinatown Gate
has welcomed visitors to the
neighborhood for several
decades, the recent addition of
the Chinatown Park *(see Parks and
Gardens)* turned the portal into a
truly majestic entrance.

As you approach the gate from the
park side, make special note of the
pattern in the pavement under
foot. The square in a circle design
symbolizes heaven and earth.

Leonard P. Zakim Bunker Hill Bridge
*North End to Charlestown across
the Charles River. www.leonard
pzakimbunkerhillbridge.org.*
Erected as part of the Big Dig *(see
box, opposite)*, the Leonard P. Zakim
Bunker Hill Bridge stretches 1,432
feet across the Charles River from
the North End to Charlestown. The
10-lane bridge—the widest cable-
stay bridge in the world—quickly
became a treasured landmark for
Bostonians. Not only does it help
ease traffic flow in the city, but its
design, suggesting a ship in full sail
is, quite simply, beautiful. Some
people love it most in full daylight,
while others think it shows off best
at night, when lights make it glow.
The name honors Lenny Zakim,
a civil rights activist who passed
away in 1999 after battling an
illness; it also commemorates the
colonists who fought at the Battle
of Bunker Hill.

⚓ Mount Auburn Cemetery
*580 Mount Auburn St., Cambridge.
617-547-7105. http://mount
auburn.org. Open daily Oct–Apr
8am–5pm, May–Aug 8am–7pm,
call for closing times the rest of the
year. Map of grounds available at
the entrance gate and the cemetery
office (open Mon–Fri 8:30am–
4:30pm, Sat until 4pm).*
Still an active burial site, Mount
Auburn Cemetery was the
country's first public large-scale
designed landscape. A National

The Big Dig: A Landmark of a Public Works Project

The Big Dig, a mammoth project fraught with delays, an ever-expanding budget and many other issues, finally wrapped up in 2007. Undertaken to relieve Boston's overwhelming traffic, the Big Dig replaced the elevated Central Artery with an underground expressway and added a new bridge and a tunnel to the city's infrastructure. Though traffic has definitely eased and 40 acres of new parks were added in and around the city, it's doubtful that Bostonians will give up debating its pros and cons (and estimated $24 billion price tag) any time soon.

Zakim Bridge

© Greater Boston CVB/FayFoto, Inc.

Historic Landmark, Mount Auburn first opened in 1831. It served as the model for the rural cemetery movement and the tradition of garden cemeteries, something that continues today.

The popularity of Mount Auburn and other garden cemeteries eventually led to the creation of the country's public park system. As much as Mount Auburn pays tribute to those buried there, it is also a place dedicated to showcasing the beauty of life. The heavily landscaped 175-acre Mount Auburn has 5,000 trees, lush gardens and a well-preserved collection of 19C buildings. Some of Boston's most prominent citizens are buried at the cemetery, including Isabella Stewart Gardner, Charles Bulfinch, Mary Baker Eddy and Henry Wadsworth Longfellow. Mount Auburn offers tours, programs and lectures about its history and horticulture throughout the year.

New England Holocaust Memorial★
Carmen Park, Congress St., near Faneuil Hall. 617 457-8755. www.nehm.com. Haymarket T stop.

Set against the backdrop of Faneuil Hall's historic buildings, the New England Holocaust Memorial's six 54-foot-tall glass towers, designed by architect Stanley Saitowitz, are particularly striking. But many visitors to the city, caught up in their exploration of the 19C or the day's shopping, don't even realize what they're seeing.

When passers-by discover that the six slender towers are more than just sidewalk sculpture, and they begin reading the inscriptions on the heavy marble slabs that bookend the memorial, then they recognize the space as a place of commemoration.

Quiet sets in quickly and continues as visitors walk through the glass towers, etched with numbers that represent the 6 million Jews who died in the Holocaust of World War II.

MUSEUMS

There's no doubt that Bostonians love to preserve (and put a spotlight on) their past, but they're also eager to showcase ideas that will take us all into the future. What better way to see both on display than at the city's museums? In just one day, you can see everything from 14C antiques to video installations that will prompt you to think about art in a whole new way.

Isabella Stewart Gardner Museum★★★

280 The Fenway. 617-566-1401. www.gardnermuseum.org. Open year-round Wed–Mon 11am–4:30pm (Thu until 8:30pm). Closed major holidays. $15 (free to anyone named Isabella!). Museum T stop.

Prepare to be enchanted! When you step inside this museum, you'll see a wealth of furnishings, textiles, paintings and sculpture collected by a woman who truly relished beauty, creativity and well, life itself. Isabella Stewart Gardner *(see sidebar, opposite)* built **Fenway Court**, which resembles a 15C Venetian-style palace, to showcase her magnificent art collection. Opening onto flower gardens in a central courtyard, the galleries,

permanently arranged by Mrs. Gardner herself, first welcomed the public in 1903.

In 2012 a new wing designed by renowned architect Renzo Piano more than doubled the museum's space, adding a lobby, cafe, gift shop, concert hall, special exhibits gallery, conservation and education studios and staff offfices.

Making the Most of the Museum

Ground Floor – Ceramic tiles from a 17C Mexican church cover the walls in the **Spanish Cloister**, setting off John Singer Sargent's dramatic painting *El Jaleo*.

The Courtyard – Lovely gardens, Venetian window frames and balconies with fresh flowers grace

Isabella Stewart Gardner Museum

MUST SEE

the courtyard. Classical sculptures surround an ancient Roman mosaic pavement (2C AD).

In the **small galleries** off the courtyard, 19C and 20C French and American paintings include portraits by Degas and Manet, and landscapes by Whistler, Matisse and Sargent. The Yellow Room houses *The Terrace, St. Tropez* (1904) by Henri Matisse, which depicts the artist's wife, dressed in a kimono.

Second Floor – The **Early Italian Rooms** contain 14C and 15C works primarily from the Renaissance. The large fresco of Hercules is the only fresco by Piero della Francesca outside Italy.

The **Raphael Room** exhibits two works of the Italian painter Raphael (1483-1520): a portrait and a pietà. *The Annunciation* (attributed to Piermatteo d'Amelia) illustrates the technique of linear perspective developed in the 15C. In the **Short Gallery**, Anders Zorn's spirited painting depicts Mrs. Gardner at her beloved haunt in Venice, the Palazzo Barbaro. The **Little Salon** showcases 18C Venetian paneling and 17C tapestries. With its 16C tapestries from France and Belgium, the **Tapestry Room** is the setting for concerts at Fenway Court. Works by Hans Holbein, Van Dyck and Rubens enliven the **Dutch Room**.

Third Floor – The **Veronese Room** features Spanish and Venetian tooled and painted leather wall coverings. The **Titian Room** contains a Titian masterpiece, painted for Philip II of Spain. In the **Long Gallery,** the life-size terra-cotta statue *Virgin Adoring the Child* provides a good example of Renaissance sculpture. *A Young Lady of Fashion*, attributed to Uccello, characterizes portrait art in 15C Florence, Italy. The **Gothic Room** holds a full-length portrait (1888) of Mrs. Gardner painted by her friend John Singer Sargent.

MUSEUMS

Museum of Fine Arts, Boston★★★

465 Huntington Ave. 617-267-9300. www.mfa.org. Open year-round daily 10am–4:45pm (Wed–Fri until 9:45pm). Closed major holidays. $25. Museum T stop.

One of the country's leading museums, the Museum of Fine Arts, Boston (MFA) boasts more than 450,000 works of art in its collections. But don't feel pressured to see them all in one day *(see Touring Tip)*. As daunting as it may seem, the museum makes visiting easy by organizing its collections into eight departments—Art of the Americas; Art of Europe; Contemporary Art; Art of Asia, Oceania and Africa; Art of the Ancient World; Prints, Drawings and Photographs; Textile and Fashion Arts; and Musical Instruments. Why not give yourself two days and see four departments per visit—or choose the areas that really interest you and concentrate on them? Free museum tours and gallery talks are included in the admission fee.

Commemorative head of a king (Oba), Edo peoples, Benin kingdom, Nigeria, late 16C, Robert Owen Lehman Collection

© Museum of Fine Arts, Boston

Touring Tip

When you buy a ticket to the MFA, it allows you one free repeat visit within 10 days. So you can return again, instead of trying to tour the entire museum in one day. Don't lose that ticket, though!

Since its founding in 1870, the Museum of Fine Arts, Boston has expanded over the decades—recently adding a new American Wing and tripling the exhibit space devoted to late 20C and Contemporary Art. The new Art of the Americas Wing opened to the public in 2010. The 50,000-square-foot space presents art from all the Americas—North, Central and South—chronologically, in 53 new galleries. Recently completed renovations also include the mid-2008 reopening of the museum's stately Fenway entrance, as well as the unveiling of the new Sharf Visitor Center. The museum's sleek and spacious Contemporary Art Wing made its debut in 2011, with seven new collection galleries.

Cream of the Collections

Art of Asia, Oceania and Africa★★★ – The MFA's **Indian Art** holdings include sculpture (2C BC–5C AD), miniature paintings from the courts of North India (16C–19C), and works of jade and ivory. **Japanese Art** showcases Buddhist and Shinto paintings and sculpture, scroll and screen paintings, ceramics, lacquerware, swords and woodblock prints. You'll also find an impressive group of **Chinese sculpture, painting and calligraphy**, as well as **Himalayan Art** from Nepal

MUST SEE

and Tibet. Ceramics and glass works from Iran, Iraq, Turkey and other Middle Eastern and North African countries highlight the **Islamic Art** collection. Korean Art holdings feature stoneware and lacquerware, Buddhist paintings and sculptures, and Bronze Age funerary objects. **Southeast Asian Art** focuses on stone and bronze sculpture, ceramics, and gold jewelry from Indonesia, Thailand and Vietnam.

American Paintings★★ –

Prominent among the 18C portraitists represented are Gilbert Stuart and John Singleton Copley (be sure to see Copley's 1768 portrait of Paul Revere). Works from America's 19C landscape painters include canvases by Fitz Hugh Lane, Albert Pinkham Ryder and Winslow Homer. The works of John Singer Sargent and Mary Cassatt, both of whom lived abroad, were largely inspired by European movements.

Ancient Egyptian, Nubian and Near Eastern Art★★ –

The MFA's collection of Egyptian art spans 4,000 years of civilization. The sculpture of **King Mycerinus** and his queen is one of the oldest existing statues portraying a couple.
Treasures from ancient Nubia (the present-day region of southern

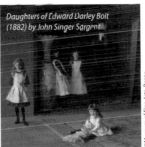

Daughters of Edward Darley Boit (1882) by John Singer Sargent

©Museum of Fine Arts, Boston

Egypt and northern Sudan) include boldly painted pottery and intricate jewelry, such as blue faience-bead necklaces (faience is a glazed ceramic made from crushed quartz or sand).
Two colossal statues of the Nubian kings stand on the second floor.

Classical Art★★ – The MFA's celebrated collection includes cameos, bronzes and Greek vases; original Greek marble sculptures; and Roman sculpture in silver and marble.

European Paintings★★ – Here you'll find works from the Middle Ages to the present. Paintings of the 16C and 17C include those of

MUSEUMS

59

El Greco and Velàzquez; the Dutch gallery boasts several works by Rembrandt, including the highly detailed *Portrait of a Woman Wearing a Gold Chain,* painted in 1634. The collection also features an impressive group of **19C French paintings** that will instantly transport you to Paris and the French countryside, including works by the Romantics (Delacroix), the realists (Courbet, Millet), the Barbizon school (Corot), the Impressionists (Renoir, Monet, Degas, Van Gogh), and the post-Impressionists (Gauguin).

Institute of Contemporary Art/ Boston★★★

100 Northern Ave. 617-478-3100. www.icaboston.org. Open year-round Tue–Sun 10am–5pm (Thu–Fri until 9pm). Closed Jan 1, Jul 4, Thanksgiving and Dec 25. $15 (free, Thu 5pm–9pm). Courthouse T stop or World Trade Center T stop.

Though the Institute of Contemporary Art (ICA)—originally the Boston Museum of Modern Art—has been around since 1936, Bostonians fell in love with it anew when it finally moved into a permanent home in December 2006. The waterfront building, a stellar piece of glass-and-metal modern architecture that quickly made fans of critics from around the world, makes marvelous use of the site's tiny .75-acre footprint. You'll marvel at the architects' ability to design a 65,000 square feet building—and one of Boston's best new destination outdoor seating areas—on such a small space.

After spending some time in front of the art wall in the lobby, which features commissioned works that

Institute of Contemporary Art/Boston

©Shorelander/Wikimedia Commons

change once a year, head straight to the **fourth floor.** That's where you'll find the ICA's 17,000 square feet of gallery space, built to make the most of the natural light that filters through the ceiling's adjustable skylight.

Year by year the ICA showcases ahead-of-the-curve creations that have included works by the likes of multimedia artist Ugo Rondinone, street artist Shepard Fairey and sculptor Charles LeDray. Recent exhibits have shown paintings by Christina Ramberg and drawings (and other work) by Barry McGee. While the media rooms at many museums aren't exactly must-sees, it's a very different story at the ICA. The Poss Family Mediatheque, an all-white room loaded with shiny white iMacs that you can use to learn more about the exhibits inside, hangs from the building's

cantilevered roof. From the room's top step, the view down through the window is all harbor (and one bright orange buoy).

It's an exciting time to get to know the ICA. They're determined to build one of the world's best collections of 21C art that will include pieces from artists they'll show throughout the century. The best places to think about the future of art—or to look over your purchases from the museum's great-gifts-for-everybody store are: a seat in the museum's glass-enclosed Water Café (you can't go wrong with the miso-glazed salmon salad) on a winter's day or, when warmer weather hits, the wooden grandstand stadium seating outside.

John F. Kennedy Presidential Library and Museum★★

Columbia Point, near University of Massachusetts, Boston. 617-514-1600. www.jfklibrary.org. Open year-round daily 9am–5pm. Closed Jan 1, Thanksgiving Day & Dec 25. $14. JFK/UMassT stop (free shuttle bus, marked JFK, from T stop to the museum every 20min from 8am to museum closing).

Architect I.M. Pei's sleek concrete-and-glass structure on the

Boston's Favorite Son

Born in Brookline, MA, John Fitzgerald Kennedy (1917–1963) grew up in a well-to-do political family, the second of nine children born to Rose Fitzgerald and Joseph Patrick Kennedy. After graduating from Harvard in 1940 and serving as an officer in the South Pacific during World War II, JFK became a congressman (1947–53) and later, a senator (1953–60). On January 20, 1961, at age 43, he became the youngest president elected in US history; two years later he was assassinated. As one of the nation's most beloved presidents, he oversaw the founding of the Peace Corps, the resolution of the Cuban missile crisis and the start of the US space program.

Atrium, John F. Kennedy Presidential Library and Museum

© Greater Boston CVB/FayFoto, Inc.

Exhibits about Jacqueline Kennedy and the restoration work she led at the White House are included. You'll leave the museum through the striking Pavilion, a nine-story glass-enclosed atrium that looks out over Boston Harbor.

Boston Children's Museum★★★
300 Congress St., Museum Wharf.
See Musts for Kids.

Museum of Science, Boston★★
Rte. 28, Science Park.
See Musts for Kids.

House Museums

Gibson House Museum★
137 Beacon St. 617-267-6338.
Open year-round by guided tour only Wed–Sun at 1pm, 2pm & 3pm. Closed major holidays. $8. Arlington T stop.

Step inside this row house designed by local architect Edward Clarke Cabot to get a sense of the reality of 19C life in Boston. Built in 1859, the Gibson House retains its Victorian flavor and, since many of the family's possessions are still inside, offers a rare glimpse into the lifestyle of an affluent Back Bay family. Your guide will walk you through daily life on the floors designed for adult use—including

waterfront serves as an elegant tribute to Boston's favorite son, John Fitzgerald Kennedy, the 35th president of the US. Inside, you'll get to know Kennedy the man, beginning with a film of his early life, narrated in JFK's own words. Immerse yourself in Kennedy's 1960 presidential campaign through film footage, including excerpts from his televised debates with Richard Nixon, and Kennedy's inaugural address. Then walk down the re-created main corridor of the White House, where rooms on either side hold exhibits relating to major events from Kennedy's presidency. In the Oval Office exhibit, look for the silver goblet Kennedy received as a present from the people of New Ross, Ireland, the city his great-grandfather sailed from when he emigrated to America.

A Remarkable Woman

Rose Standish Nichols was born in 1872. She lived during an age when women were expected to marry and have children. Miss Nichols, however, chose another path. To support herself, she worked as a landscape gardener. But her talents didn't end there; she also excelled in woodworking and needlepoint. During her long life (she died in 1960 at age 88), she was both a suffragette and a women's-rights activist. An avid pacifist, she assisted in founding the Woman's International League for Peace and Freedom in 1915.

MUST SEE

the original kitchen—and into the children's domain, on the fourth floor. After you see the elaborate woodwork, 15-foot ceilings, imported carpets, mock leather wallpaper and plenty of curios, you'll agree that the Gibson family had both taste, and the money to display it. Please note that the tour travels up four floors of the house but there is no elevator.

Nichols House Museum★
55 Mount Vernon St. 617-227-6993. www.nicholshousemuseum.org. Open Apr–Oct Tue–Sat 11am–4pm. Rest of the year Thu–Sat 11am–4pm. Tours every half hour beginning at 11am. Closed major holidays. $8. Park St. T stop.

Don't miss this opportunity to peek inside a home with a Beacon Hill address. This little brick beauty was designed by Charles Bulfinch, the architect of the State House (and the man behind the Otis House, below), and completed in 1804. The four-story town house preserves the possessions and the colorful spirit of Rose Standish Nichols *(see sidebar below, opposite)*. In the spacious interior you'll see such finery as late-19C and early-20C furniture carved by Miss Nichols herself, as well as Flemish tapestries, ancestral paintings and sculptures that she collected on her numerous trips abroad. Look for examples of her needlepoint in the bedroom. While many historic homes feel, well, a bit cold, the Nichols House has a cozy feel you won't soon forget.

Otis House
141 Cambridge St. 617-994-5920. www.historicnewengland.org. Open year-round by guided tour only Wed–Sun 11am–4:30pm. Closed major holidays. $8. At the foot of Beacon Hill, close to the Charles St./MGH, Bowdoin Square, or Government Center T stops.

Built in 1796, the house was designed by two of the men most responsible for the look of Boston's cityscape: architect Charles Bulfinch and Harrison Gray Otis, a lawyer, speculator and politician (and the developer behind Beacon Hill). While the Federal-style dwelling may look a bit severe to some, notice that Bulfinch softened it by including a second story Palladian window in the design. Inside, the exquisite period furniture, ornate moldings, and hand-blocked borders will make it clear that late-18C Bostonians had rather refined taste.

Also serving as the headquarters of the Historic New England organization, the Otis House is the starting point for walking tours of Beacon Hill.

Cooper-Frost-Austin House
21 Linnaean St., Cambridge. 617-994-6669. www.historicnew england.org. $5. The house has very limited tour dates that change each year; contact Historic New England for schedule (contact information is shown under Otis House).

You can tour the Cooper-Frost-Austin House only two or three days each summer but, if you're in town when it's open, head over. The oldest dwelling still standing in Cambridge, the "half house" structure first went up in 1681; it was enlarged in both the early 1700s and 1800s. It's early American housing at its most interesting.

MUSEUMS

PARKS AND GARDENS

Boston boasts the oldest public garden in America, a 34-island National Park Recreation Area, and a well-designed string of greenways and leafy malls encircling the city. When visiting, do as the locals do: take your time. Stroll the tree-lined promenades, hike the trails of a rocky island, spread a blanket in the park and smell the flowers. Here are Boston's not-to-be-missed green spaces and pretty places.

Boston Public Garden

© Greater Boston CVB/FayFoto, Inc.

Boston Public Garden★★

Bounded by Arlington, Boylston, Charles & Beacon Sts. 617-723-8144. www.friendsofthepublic garden.org.

This 24-acre rectangular park, bordered by a handsome cast-iron fence, was reclaimed from the swampy Back Bay in the 1830s for the purpose of creating a botanical garden. Today the popular retreat will enchant you with its flowering parterres, tree-lined footpaths, fountains and commemorative statuary. Drooping willows, blooming dogwoods and fragrant cherry trees flank formal beds of roses and lilies and fiery displays of brightly colored annuals. The centerpiece of the garden is the bridge that crosses the large lagoon. Here, visitors line up to

Make Way for Ducklings

© Greater Boston CVB/FayFoto, Inc.

Public Garden, northeast section, Arlington T stop. See Musts for Kids. The Public Garden is home to the cutest pieces of bronze in the city, the ducklings immortalized in Robert McCloskey's classic children's book, *Make Way for Ducklings* (1941). Combine a visit to the ducklings with a ride on the swan boats for a perfect, pint-size piece of Boston history. For a bigger slice, try a Boston by Little Feet tour, geared to children *(see Musts for Kids).*

MUST SEE

Touring Tip

Check out the equestrian statue of George Washington at the Arlington Street gate. The statue, sculpted by Thomas Ball in 1878, is the first to show Washington on a horse. Follow George's gaze and you'll be looking up the perfectly aligned and beautiful Commonwealth Avenue★★ (see Neighborhoods, Back Bay).

board the famous foot-pedaled **swan boats**. You'll want to, too (see Musts for Kids).

If you would rather learn something as you look around, contact the Friends of the Public Garden (617-723-8144) to arrange a history or horticulture tour (also available for the Boston Common and Commonwealth Avenue Mall). Keep in mind: the Public Garden (and, actually, all of Boston's parks) is a great year-round place to play (or stroll). The swan boats make way for ice skates come winter (see Musts for Fun) and, no matter how old you are, one of Boston's big snowfalls is the perfect excuse to head out for a romp in the white powder. Just don't forget boots.

Arnold Arboretum★

125 Arborway, Jamaica Plain. 617-524-1718. www.arboretum. harvard.edu. Grounds open year-round daily dawn–dusk. Visitor center open Apr–Oct Thu–Tue 10am–4pm; rest of the year Thu–Tue noon–4pm. Orange Line to Forest Hills station. Maps are available at the guardhouse.

This 281-acre arboretum is serious stuff. It's an outdoor research/educational facility run by Harvard University and the Department of Parks and Recreation. But all you need for your visit is an appreciation of beauty and a good pair of walking shoes.

Touring Tip

Try one or all of these suggested walks, which take about 15 minutes each. Ask for a map of the grounds as you enter the arboretum.

♦ Jamaica Plain Gate to the pond area
♦ Pond area to the Bonsai House
♦ Bonsai House to Bussey Hill, where there's a panorama of the arboretum.

Arnold Arboretum

© Greater Boston CVB/FayFoto, Inc.

PARKS AND GARDENS

Boston Gets Greener

As a result of The Big Dig (see Landmarks), more parks opened in 2005 than had been opened since the time of Frederick Law Olmsted. Among the new riverfront parks are North Point, Nashua Meadows and Paul Revere Landing, plus the nearly complete 47-mile Boston Harborwalk (*www.bostonharborwalk.com*), from the JFK Library to the suburb of Winthrop.

Founded in 1872, the arboretum has evolved into a living museum of about 7,000 species of ornamental trees and shrubs. The place is especially delightful in May and June when the delicate scents of blooming lilacs, azaleas, rhododendrons and magnolias fill the air.

Back Bay Fens★
Fenway Park Dr. 617-635-4500. www.cityofboston.gov/parks. Open year-round daily 7:30am–dusk. Green Line E train to Museum of Fine Arts T stop.

This park is tucked behind Boston's Museum of Fine Arts—and it's like entering a different world. Part of the Olmsted-designed Emerald Necklace *(see p 69)*, the urban oasis is surrounded by highways and high rises, but within it, you'll discover a peaceful haven. It's a popular place; people come here to bird-watch (you might spot songbirds and snowy egrets), play ball on one of the fields, jog along the running circuit or tend to their gardens. The park boasts one of the oldest Victory Gardens in the country, started during World War

II. Today there are hundreds of plots planted and maintained by locals. Become a part of the gardening community, at least for a day, at the Fenway Victory Gardens Fens Fest (call or go online for the date, *www.fenwayvictorygardens.com).* Another highlight is the Kellecher Rose Garden (a popular spot for Bostonian weddings), enclosed by a hemlock hedge.

Boston Common★
Bordered by Boylston, Tremont, Park & Beacon Sts.

You can't (and shouldn't) miss Boston Common. Smack dab in the center of town, this public park claims a whopping 50 acres. It's a popular gathering spot for dog walkers, joggers, cart vendors, studying students and families and yes, a fair amount of homeless people. Whereas the Public Garden is quiet and contained, the adjacent Common is open and bustling. The oldest park in the country, the Common has belonged to the people of Boston since the 1630s, when Reverend Blackstone sold the tract to the Puritans. Designated by these early Bostonians as "Common Field" forever reserved for public use, this landmark has served over the centuries as pastureland, a military training ground, public execution site and concert venue. The **Central Burying Ground** (1756) fronting Boylston Street contains the unmarked grave of Gilbert Stuart, the early-American portraitist who painted the likeness of George Washington that appears on the US one-dollar bill. **Frog Pond** is a beloved winter spot for skating *(see Musts for Fun).*

Charles River Reservation★

Stretches 20 miles along Boston Harbor. 617-626-1250. www.mass.gov/dcr/parks/charlesRiver.

Activities along the 20-mile Charles River Reservation could keep you occupied the entire time you're in Boston. Biking, kayaking, wildlife watching—it's all there. Landscaped in the early 1930s, the bustling waterfront park attracts joggers, in-line skaters, picnickers and sailing enthusiasts. The lower half, the Charles River Basin, stretches from downtown Boston all the way up to the Watertown Dam, and includes the Esplanade. The upper section starts at Watertown Square and goes to Riverdale Park in West Roxbury. If you're going to explore only one section of the Reservation, head to the Esplanade. Access it by the Fiedler Footbridge at the corner of Beacon and Arlington streets. If you're visiting in summertime, catch an outdoor performance at the **Hatch Memorial Shell** *(off Storrow Dr.; see Musts for Fun).*

Other highlights of the Charles River Reservation include:

Artesani Playground – *1255 Soldiers Field Rd., Brighton.* Cool off in the spray pool or wading area at this, the largest playground on the 20-mile stretch.

Nashua Street Park – *200 Nashua St.* There's no better place to go for a good view of the elegant Zakim Bunker Hill Bridge (one of the most beautiful structures built during the Big Dig) than this 2-acre riverfront park. Take a seat on one of the granite stones known as "The Eggs."

Forest Hills Cemetery★

95 Forest Hills Ave., Jamaica Plain. 617-524-0128. www.foresthills cemetery.com. Open year-round daily dawn–dusk. Orange Line to Forest Hills station.

More than 150 years old, this rural cemetery garden is one of the prettiest in the country, nationally known for its collection of memorial sculpture and handsome Victorian landscape. You can stroll the more than 275-acre grounds, through stately groves of trees and around a small pond, enjoying scenic vistas along the way. Many prominent figures are buried at the still-functioning cemetery, including suffragist Lucy Stone, playwright Eugene O'Neill, and poets Anne Sexton and e.e. cummings.

Pond in Boston Common

PARKS AND GARDENS

Boston Harbor Islands★

617-223-8666. www.boston islands.com. Ferries & tour boats operate mid-May–mid-Oct daily. See also Musts for Fun.

Imagine a lush, nearly deserted island where you can wander, play in the surf and paddle to your heart's content. Now, imagine that same idyllic spot is a mere eight miles from a major metropolitan area. Picture that, and you've got a sense of the Boston Harbor Islands, a National Recreation Area, where nature meets man-made cityscape, separated by a splash of blue water. The area includes 34 islands, ranging in size from 214 acres to less than one acre, each with its own colorful, often bloody history, as sites of early European settlements, Revolutionary War skirmishes, Civil War forts, and prison compounds. Today they offer splendid scenery and an easy escape from the noisy city streets. Ranger-led tours, concerts, theater, children's activities and boat cruises are offered on many of the islands throughout the season.

Boston Flower Show

Just when New Englanders can barely stand the dreary winter weather, the flower show comes to town! Touted as the third-largest flower show in the world, the Boston Flower & Garden Show is typically held in March, filling the massive Bayside Exposition Center (200 Mt. Vernon St.) with over-the-top flower, landscape and garden displays. *For information, contact the Massachusetts Horticultural Society: 617-933-4900; www.masshort.org.*

Rose Fitzgerald Kennedy Greenway★

1 mile of connected parks that link Chinatown, Dewey Square, the Wharf District and the North End. 617-292-0020. www.rosekennedy greenway.org. Open year-round daily 7am–11pm (pedestrians may cross the parks at any time). For Chinatown and Dewey Square, South Station T stop; for the Wharf District, Aquarium T stop, for the North End, Haymarket T stop.

If you haven't been to Boston in a few years, get ready for some big changes. Though the Big Dig *(see Landmarks)* was one of the priciest public works projects in US history, the results quieted Bostonian grumbling quite a bit. The city spent some of those greenbacks adding gorgeous green space around the city *(see sidebar p 66)*, most notably the Rose Fitzgerald Kennedy Greenway. Space for the one-mile stretch of linked parks opened up when the Big Dig took down one of Boston's most traffic-filled roads, the elevated Central Artery. Now, instead of bumper-to-bumpering your way along the route, you can stroll, relax, play and inhale the scent of the fresh flowers and foliage along the way. Each park on the Greenway has a distinct personality and features that play into the neighborhood it borders. The **Chinatown Park**, which sits right outside the neighborhood's famous gated entrance, was designed following the principles of Feng Shui, including balance and harmony. At **Dewey Square Park**, commuters who pass through nearby South Station finally have a place where they can take a breather in the midst of their busy work day.

MUST SEE

In the 3-acre **North End Parks**, the open space encourages visitors to ponder all the historic sites in the area; the Freedom Trail runs right through it. And part of the **Wharf District Park**, celebrating its by-the-harbor location, has a nautical theme.

The best way to explore the Greenway? Start in Chinatown. Pick up a Vietnamese *bánh mì* sandwich at **Lu's Sandwich Shop** *(15 Beach St.)* for just $2.50 each—the BBQ beef is a must--they're the tastiest food bargain in Boston.

Picnic in the park and then amble along, with frequent stops to test out all the park benches, until you reach the North End.

By that time, you'll need another snack. Finish up with an espresso and a florentine lace cookie (the big one, with nuts) at **Modern Pastry** *(257 Hanover St.; www. modernpastry.com).*

The Emerald Necklace

Open daily year-round. Emerald Necklace Conservancy's Shattuck Visitor Center at 125 The Fenway; open May–Oct Mon–Fri 9am–6pm, Sun noon–4pm; rest of the year Mon–Fri 9am–6pm. 617-522-2700. www.emeraldnecklace.org.

Take a look at a map *(see inside front cover)* of Boston and you'll see a strand of green running through the city. Known as "The Emerald Necklace," this urban jewel encompasses six parks and more than 1,000 acres of public land, extending five miles from the Charles River to Dorchester.

The greenway—which includes the Back Bay Fens, Riverway, Olmsted Park, Jamaica Park, Arnold Arboretum and Franklin Park—was designed by Frederick Law Olmsted, Sr., America's first landscape architect.

Today Boston's Emerald Necklace is listed on the National Register of Historic Places as the only remaining intact linear park designed by Olmsted.

PARKS AND GARDENS

© Rose Kennedy Greenway Conservancy/
Courtesy of the Greater Boston CVB

North End Park, Rose Fitzgerald Kennedy Greenway

FOR FUN

Boston may be better known as a history and culture spot than an outdoorsy paradise, but the city—and its surrounding area—offers plenty of places to play. Some things are so truly Boston, you just shouldn't miss them. Even been-there-done-that residents are secretly pleased to relive these experiences when out-of-towners come to visit. The following are all local favorites.

♨ Attend a Concert on the Esplanade

Outdoor concerts on the **Charles River Esplanade**★, the grassy area along the banks on the Boston side of the Charles River (*see Parks and Gardens*), are a local tradition. Look for the **Hatch Memorial Shell**, a band shell, off Storrow Drive (*see inside cover map*). Also at this venue, the Boston Pops offers a week of free outdoor concerts in summer, including the **Boston Pops Fireworks Spectacular** ♨, its famous, televised-around-the-planet, **Fourth of July** performance, complete with patriotic songs and fireworks. The annual event draws upwards of a half a million people, who stake out their spot on the grass in the early morning for their blanket. Some dress in red-white-and-blue costumes and wave small US flags during the performance.

Sing at Singing Beach★

119 Beach St., Manchester-by-the-Sea. 29mi northeast of Boston. Take I-95 N to Rte. 128 N. At Exit 16 (the Pine St./Manchester exit) take Rte. 127 one-quarter mile into Manchester-by-the-Sea. Limited parking; on Fri–Sun, parking at Singing Beach is for residents only. Also reachable by commuter rail from North Station, Rockport line. 978-527-2000. www.manchester.ma.us. Bathhouse open daily 9am–7pm in summer.

Set in the upscale North Shore community of Manchester-by-the-Sea, Singing Beach is easily accessible from Boston, thanks to the commuter rail. Bring your beach chair, a towel and a small cooler, but not much more in the way of gear, as you'll be walking about a mile to the beach from the train stop! It's worth it, though; this lovely stretch of beach gets

Singing Beach

©Chee-Onn Leong/Dreamstime.com

MUST DO

its name because it "sings" (okay, it squeaks) when you walk on it. On the way back to the train, stop at **Captain Dusty's** (60 Beach St.; 978-526-1663) for an ice-cream cone and enjoy it in Masconomo Park, across the street.

Revel at Revere Beach ★

Revere Beach Blvd., Revere. 5.5mi northeast of Boston. Take Rte. 1A north past Logan Airport to Revere. Turn right onto Oak Island St. and continue to the beach. Or ride the MBTA Blue Line Revere Beach or Wonderland T stop. 978-535-7205. www.reverebeach.com.

More than just another sandy swatch, Revere Beach is a National Historic Landmark and America's first public ocean beach. Designed by renowned landscape architect Charles Eliot, it has an old-time charm, thanks to its still-standing pavilions, bandstand and promenade. This is the first beach you'll encounter north of town, and it gets a colorful crowd, ranging from pre-teens in toe rings and thong bikinis to, well, grandparents in toe rings and thong bikinis! The annual *(mid-Jul)* **New England Sand Sculpting Festival** shows off some amazing creations in sand *(www.reverebeach partnership.com).*

Bike or Skate the Emerald Necklace

When it comes to cycling, Boston's streets are best left to the daredevil bike couriers. A good option for all other riders is the 18-mile **Dr. Paul Dudley White Bikeway**, which loops between Science Park and Watertown. This is a multi-use trail, so etiquette dictates that cyclists stay closer to the road than the

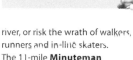

river, or risk the wrath of walkers, runners and in-line skaters. The 11-mile **Minuteman Commuter Bikeway**— "America's Revolutionary Rail-Trail"—follows inactive railroad tracks from the Alewife T (subway) station, at the end of the Red Line in North Cambridge, through the towns of Arlington, Lexington and Bedford. Download a trail map at www.minutemanbikeway.org. Don't plan to put the pedal to the metal on this one; on weekends, it's well-used by the joggers-with-babies and tots-on-training-wheels set.

FOR FUN

Heating Up the Ice

Sure, the Red Sox-Yankees rivalry is legendary. But the all-Boston (and, well, Cambridge) rivalry between the ice hockey teams at Boston University, Boston College, Harvard and Northeastern is just as exciting. Every February, watch them fight for bragging rights at the annual Beanpot Tournament *(TD Garden; www.beanpothockey.com)*. Not in town for the Beanpot? Check team schedules to see a regular season game.

🏛 Catch a Red Sox Game at Fenway Park

4 Yawkey Way. Regular season games played Apr–Oct. 617-267-8661. http://boston.redsox.mlb.com. Kenmore T stop.

Think Bostonians are prim and proper? You've never been to a Red Sox game. Or in particular, a Red Sox-New York Yankees game, where jeers yelled out by Sox fans would make many a proper Bostonian blush. (Or, at least, that's what they would claim. They're probably out there yelling, too.) Red Sox fever shot sky high in 2004 when the team won the World Series and broke the Curse of the Bambino (Babe Ruth, of course). Sox fans had waited—some more patiently than others—86 years for a championship win. The team proved it was no one-time fluke by taking the title again in 2007 and again in 2013.

Built in 1912, outdoor Fenway Park is America's oldest ballpark, and home of the famed **Green Monster**, the 37-foot-high left-field wall that rises a batter-testing 310 feet from home plate. You'll be as charmed as the die-hard fans, who love their historic stadium as much as the team itself.

🏛 Go Whale Watching

Boston Harbor Cruises depart from Central Wharf. Apr–Oct. 617-227-4321. www.bostonharbor cruises.com. $46. Aquarium T stop. Boston Harbor Cruises also operates the New England Aquarium Whale Watch cruises departing from Central Wharf Apr–Oct. 617-973-5206. www.neaq.org. $47. Aquarium T stop. Advance reservations recommended.

Night game, Fenway Park

Greater Boston CVB/FayFoto, Inc.

MUST DO

Humpback whale in Stellwagen Bank National Marine Sanctuary

©Jose Gil/Bigstockphoto.com

"Finner at four o'clock!" isn't exactly "Thar she blows!" but you'll get the idea. Seeing whales in the wild is always a thrill—and it's easy to do. The cruise takes you about 30 miles off the coast of Boston to Stellwagen Bank, an underwater plateau at the heart of the 842-square-mile **Stellwagen Bank National Marine Sanctuary** (http://stellwagen.noaa.gov). Whales pass by en route from the Caribbean north to Greenland and Newfoundland.

The area is a popular feeding ground for migrating whales, including humpbacks, fin whales and minke whales. (Dolphins and harbor seals—always a favorite with kids—also make regular appearances in the area.)

Cruises last three to four hours. Along the way, on board naturalists point out marine life and discuss the whales' feeding, breeding and migration patterns. A whale or two might even show off for you by coming close to the boat, breaching (think leaping) or spyhopping (it's like the whale version of treading water). Keep the camera handy.

Ice Skate on Frog Pond

Boston Common. 617-635-2120; www.bostonfrogpond.com. $5. Park Street T stop.

"Wintah" in Boston can be positively magical, especially at Frog Pond. When the **Boston Common★** *(see Parks and Gardens)* is dressed in twinkling lights and the ice is sufficiently solid, loads of people lace up skates for an outing right out of Currier & Ives. You can rent skates *($9)*, enjoy concession treats like hot cocoa, and take a break in the warming hut.

Island Hop Boston Style

Ferries depart from Long Wharf (parking available) to Georges and Spectacle Islands. 617-223-8666. www.bostonharborislands.org.

Touring Tip

You can buy food on the ships. But bring more warm clothes than you think you'll need (it can be 20 degrees colder on the open water), sunscreen, a hat, binoculars and, if rough water gets to you, seasickness medication.

FOR FUN

73

Ice skating on Frog Pond

© Gwen Cannon/Michelin

Aquarium T stop. For ferry information, contact Boston's Best Cruises (617-777-0040; www.bostonsbestcruises.com). $15 adults, $9 children (ages 4–11), or $43 per family (2 adults and 2 children).

If you flew into Boston, you may have noticed the 34 little green islands that comprise the Boston Harbor Islands *(see Parks and Gardens)*, a National Recreation Area. Why not get a closer view by boat and on foot? The islands offer outdoor adventures a-plenty, including hiking and kayaking, as well as quiet picnic spots, old ruins, and dazzling views of the city. Green-minded travelers will get a kick out of Spectacle Island. (And everybody enjoys learning the story behind the island's name:

European settlers back in 1630 thought its two hills—connected by a sandbar—looked like a pair of giant spectacles.) Used as a garbage dump from the 1920s until 1959, the island was rehabilitated with dirt and gravel displaced in the Big Dig. The island, along with its renewable energy-run visitor center, opened to the public in 2005. On warm days, don't forget your bathing suit; the beach is a swimmer's delight. Want to really get to know the Harbor Islands? Consider camping out on Grape, Bumpkin, Peddocks or Lovells Islands. *Connecting ferries available from Georges Island. No fresh water available on Grape, Bumpkin or Lovells Islands; pack-in/pack-out policies in effect. Reservations strongly recommended. 617-223-8666, or*

Touring Tip

If you want shell beaches, wildflower trails and campsites, go to 30-acre **Bumpkin Island**. For a diverse landscape, including a marsh and coastal forests, it's off to **Peddocks Island** you go. For Boston's skyline and history to boot, **Gallops Island** offers city views and historic ruins. And 100-acre **Spectacle Island** has a marina, a visitor center, two beaches and five miles of trails. Take your pick!

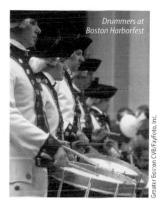

Drummers at Boston Harborfest

Greater Boston CVB/FayFoto, Inc.

877-422-6762 (camping reservations) www.reserveamerica.com. Campsites for 1–4 people are, per night, $8 for Massachusetts residents, $10 non-residents,

Have Fun Year-Round

There's always a festival or big event going on in Boston, even in the dead of winter. Here are some standouts. *For details, Greater Boston Convention and Visitors Center (CVB) 888-733-2678; www.bostonusa.com or www.cityofboston.gov/calendar.*

Chinese New Year – *Late January or early February.* The Chinese festival of the lunar new year brings dragonboat parades (and firecrackers) to Chinatown.

St. Patrick's Day Parade – *March 17 (call CVB for actual date of parade).* Everybody's Irish, if just for a day, and hanging out on Broadway Street in Southie (South Boston) to watch this parade.

Opening Day at Fenway Park – *Early April.* Red Sox opening day marks the true start of spring for BoSox fans.

Boston Marathon *Patriots' Day, 3rd Monday in April. www.baa. org.* The crowds line the street to cheer the runners in the world's oldest annual marathon.

Boston Harborfest – *Early July. 617-227-1528. www.boston harborfest.com.* Every summer, in the days surrounding July 4th, Boston's harbor turns into festival central as Bostonians celebrate Harborfest. Activities include a chowderfest and the annual turnaround cruise of the USS *Constitution*. The celebration ends with a bang—literally— when the Boston Pops plays a concert in **Hatch Memorial Shell** on the **Charles River Esplanade★** *(see Parks and Gardens),* punctuated by a grand fireworks display.

Saints' Feasts – *June to September. www.northendboston. com.* Italians in the North End, Boston's Little Italy, traditionally celebrate the feast days of many saints. Festivals like Saint Rocco, Saint Joseph, Madonna Della Cava and the Blessing of the Waters add color and drama to summer—not to mention food vendors and local restaurants offering irresistible eats.

Head of the Charles Regatta – *Mid- to late October. www. hocr.org.* Held in Cambridge, the Head of the Charles is the biggest two-day rowing event in the world (and a Boston tradition, to boot).

Thanksgiving at Plimoth Plantation – *Last Thursday in November.* Call 508-746-1622 for details and dinner reservations. *www.plimoth.org.* What better place to enjoy Thanksgiving than the place where the first Thanksgiving dinner was held? Pass the cornbread stuffing, please.

First Night Boston – *December 31.* 857-600-1590. www.firstnightboston. org. Take your pick from more than 250 indoor and outdoor exhibitions and performances during this city-wide—and family friendly—New Year's Eve festival. First Night Boston features ice sculptures, a parade, fireworks and artsy activities galore.

Pack a Picnic

It's hard to imagine **Boston Common★** *(see Parks and Gardens)* as it used to be, when Bostonians grazed cattle here, and later, when British soldiers used the common as a training ground prior to the Revolutionary War. Now, this urban park—along with the **Boston Public Garden★★**, across Charles Street—is an oasis of green in the heart of the city. In summer the

Common is the setting for free open-air concerts and Shakespeare plays, while the manicured and flower-bedecked Public Garden has a more genteel feel. Find a spot on the lawn and settle in for some picnicking and people-watching. Pick up picnic provisions at nearby **DeLuca's Market** *(11 Charles St.; 617-523-4343; www.delucasmarket.com)* or to make a day of it, shop your way through the Italian markets in the **North End** first *(see Neighborhoods)* to gather goodies that will make picnic passersby drool with envy.

Paddle the Charles River

Two parking lots off Soldier's Field Rd.; look for the green-roof kiosk. By subway, take Red Line to Harvard T stop. Take no. 86 bus to Smith's Playground and walk across the playground by Harvard Stadium and out to Soldier's Field Rd. Cross the street and walk 100 yards to the right. Rentals available from Charles River Canoe & Kayak. 617-965-5110. www.paddleboston.com.

Slip a canoe or kayak into the Charles River and enjoy one of

Kayaking on the Charles River

© A.P. Cortizas Jr./iStockphoto.com

Wild Blue Yonder

Southeast of the city, **Blue Hills Reservation** boasts (in Boston speak) "wicked awesome" views of the city. At 635 feet, Great Blue Hill, one of 22 peaks in the Blue Mountain chain, is the highest point on the Atlantic coast south of Maine. Okay, so it's not lofty, but it's fun to hike! The 10-mile Skyline Trail connects the nine peaks of the reservation. Shorter trails, some suitable for hiking with children, feature stone walls, sandy bogs and sun-dappled stands of hemlock and pine. Cool off at Houghtons Pond, a spring-fed kettle pond that's a favorite local swimming hole. Pick up a trail map at the headquarters or download it before you go (695 Hillside St., Milton; 617-698-1802; www.mass.gov; open year-round daily dawn to dusk).

the most scenic sections of urban river in the country. Lined with parklands, the Charles River basin is part of the **Emerald Necklace** (see Parks and Gardens) of green space designed by Frederick Law Olmstead.

Rent a canoe or kayak, or BYOB (bring your own boat). Head upriver and glide past peaceful shores lined with willow trees; head downriver and find a different view of the city, framed by arched bridges.

Dine with a View

Put a new spin on multi-tasking by taking in a stellar view of the city while eating a meal. The well-named **Top of the Hub** (Prudential Center, 800 Boylston St.; 617-536-1775; www.topofthehub.net) entices diners with innovative American cuisine and breathtaking panoramas of Boston from the 52nd floor of the Prudential Center.

Meritage, an upscale, elegant restaurant within Boston Harbor Hotel (70 Rowes Wharf; 617-439-3995; www.meritagetherestaurant.com) offers lovely harbor views and inspired food/wine pairings. You can also get a gaze-all-day river view with your meal at **Riverview**

Café in the **Museum of Science, Boston** (1 Science Park; 617-723-2500; www.mos.org; see Musts for Kids).

Romp at 🏕 Wompatuck State Park

204 Union St., Hingham. 19 miles south of Boston. Take I 93/Rte. 3 south to Exit 14; then take Rte. 228 north 5 miles to Free St. Turn right and drive 1 mile. Park entrance is on the right. 781-749-7160. www.mass.gov. Camping season stretches from mid-Apr to late-Oct.

When you've had enough of city sounds and sights, there's nothing like the pine-scented woodlands of a nearby state park. Just 19 miles southeast of Boston, Wompatuck is a favorite of cyclists, boasting 12 miles of paved paths and another 30 miles or so of unpaved, multi-use trails. These routes wind through lush forests and alongside freshwater ponds.

Skip hauling in too much water: you can refill your bottles from the naturally fresh H2O of Mount Blue Spring. Some 262 campsites (some with, some without, electricity) beckon you to stay for a day or two. If the idea appeals, reserve one in advance.

FOR KIDS

Boston loves kids, and the feeling is mutual! The city is exciting, it's easy to walk around, and it's brimming with family-friendly attractions, museums and fun-to-visit sights. From the swan boats in Boston Public Garden to the world-class Museum of Science and the hands-on exhibits of the Children's Museum, Beantown has plenty for families with kids of all ages to see and do.

Boston Children's Museum

Karin Hansen/Boston Children's Museum

Boston Children's Museum★★★

Museum Wharf, 308 Congress St. 617-426-8855. www.boston childrensmuseum.org. Open year-round daily 10am–5pm (Fri until 9pm). Closed Thanksgiving Day & Dec 25. $14 (ages 1 and older), free under age one. $1 Fri 5pm–9pm. Red Line to South Station T stop or Silver Line to Courthouse Station T stop.

It's clear from the get-go that the Boston Children's Museum isn't a look-but-don't-touch kind of place. Instead, the bustling multilevel museum (which deserves a full day or two of your family's time) is all about *please do touch*—and run and giggle (while, all along the way, learning a thing or five). As soon as you turn over your tickets, your kids will be off and zipping up the climbing sculpture that

What's in the Milk Bottle?

That 40-foot tall Hood milk bottle sitting in front of the museum isn't just a fun sight to see. It's a (warm weather only) food kiosk. Order some ice cream or a kid-friendly lunch through the service window. Then, sit at one of the picnic tables parked around it. Your family is sure to vote it one of the best al fresco eating spots in town.

stretches three floors up from the lobby. Environmentally-minded kids will cheer over the museum's green ways. Following a complete renovation (it reopened in 2007), the museum was the first in Boston to get LEED gold certification from the US Building Council.

MUST DO

78

Though the museum is best suited to ages 1 to 10, kids ages 11 to 13 will feel right at home on Friday evenings, 5pm to 9pm, when the entrance fee is $1.

For the 0 to 3 Years Set

Parents of the under-3 crowd should take their tots straight to **Playspace**, a museum within the museum. The section was designed to give wee ones a place where they can explore at their own pace. Young walkers can cross bridges and take a turn on slides in the tree house climber, get messy on the see-through painting wall, or play with the massive toy train set. Crawlers will find soft comfort in the infant area. *Open Sat–Thu 10am–4:30pm, Fri until 8:30pm.*

For Ages 4 and Older

In the **Investigate** exhibit, kids can engage in activities designed to stimulate and reinforce scientific inquiry; build their own woodworking project at **Johnny's Workbench**; get up close to a working artist in **The Gallery**; and light up the interactive dance floor of **Kid Power.** But wait, there's more: your kids can also walk through a real 100-year-old silk merchant's home that was donated by Boston's sister city, Kyoto; visit **Arthur the Aardvark**; and appear in their own TV show.

Museum of Science, Boston★★

Rte. 28, 1 Science Park. 617-723-2500. www.mos.org. Open year-round daily 9am–5pm (Fri until 9pm). Extended summer hours: Sat–Thu open until 7pm. Closed Thanksgiving Day & Dec 25. $23 adults, $20 children (ages 3–11). Combination tickets available for museum, Omni Theatre and Hayden Planetarium. Green Line to Science Park T stop.

More than 600 interactive exhibits, a planetarium and observatory, and a theater with a five-story screen greet you when you visit this highly regarded museum along the Charles River. Here children can explore science and technology through cutting-edge, hands-on exhibits. Push-button displays and life-size models make it easy to participate in

© Michael Malyszko

Butterfly Garden, Museum of Science, Boston

FOR KIDS

The 440-foot-long spray pool at Frog Pond on Boston Common *(see Parks and Gardens)* is a great place for a summer cool-down. The shallow water, just 6 to 18 inches deep, makes a fine wading spot for little ones; older kids love to stand under the bubbling fountain. Lifeguards are on duty, concessions are nearby, and picnic tables have umbrellas. Even swim diapers (required for toddlers) are available at the concession stand. Come winter, Frog Pond is a favorite spot for ice skating *(see Musts for Fun)*.

such activities as playing with lightning produced by a Van de Graaff generator, or "flying" through the cosmos in models of American spacecraft. You can also watch butterflies, see new chicks hatch, peer through the world's largest magnifying glass, and gaze at galaxies and quasars at the **Charles Hayden Planetarium**. When you first arrive, check the schedule to see what live exhibitions are planned throughout the day. They're often (literally) quite electric!

The Great Outdoors

The Massachusetts Department of Conservation and Recreation (DCR) website provides plenty of information about multiple kid- and family-friendly facilities and programs throughout the Boston area; it's a great planning tool. The site includes links to state parks in the area; trail maps; ranger activities and educational programs in addition to annual event listings and outdoor recreation opportunities. *Contact the Massachusetts Dept. Conservation and Recreation (www.mass.gov/eea).*

Boston Public Garden for Kids

Bounded by Arlington, Boylston, Charles & Beacon Sts. Green Line to Arlington T stop. See Parks and Gardens.

Sure, this popular city oasis is pretty, but who cares if you're a kid? The star attraction for families is the famous **swan boats**, an enduring symbol of Boston. These fanciful, pedal-powered boats have been delighting visitors and locals since 1877. As the oh-so-slow watercraft move across the Public Garden **Lagoon**, friendly ducks trail along looking for handouts. The garden is the setting for Robert McCloskey's well-known book *Make Way for Ducklings*, the classic children's story of a mallard family looking for a home.

After the ride, have your children search for the **bronze replicas** of the story's characters that are scattered in the park; it's a popular place for a family photo as well. *Swan boats depart from the pavilion in the center of the garden (mid-Apr–mid-Sept daily 10am–4pm, until 5pm in summer months; $3 adults, $1.50 children ages 2–15; 617-522-1966; www.swanboats.com).*

New England Aquarium ★★★

Central Wharf, off Atlantic Ave. 617-973-5200. www.neaq.org. Open year-round Mon–Fri 9am–5pm, weekends 9am–6pm. Extended summer hours: Sun–Thu open until 6pm, Fri–Sat open until 7pm. Closed Thanksgiving Day & Dec 25. Aquarium: $24.95 adults, $17.95 children (ages 3–11). IMAX: $9.95 adults, $7.95 children. Combination tickets are available for Aquarium & IMAX. Blue Line to Aquarium T stop.

Touring Tip

The aquarium also offers whale-watching cruises on which naturalists provide running commentary, and sightings are guaranteed *(depart mid-Apr–Oct, for information and reservations, call 617-973-5206 or visit www.neaq.org; for more on whale-watching excursions, see Musts for Fun).*

Perched on Boston's pretty waterfront, this four-story, glass and stainless-steel spiral aquarium is one of the city's most beloved attractions. Where else can you see fish with glow-in-the-dark eyeballs, rare Australian sea dragons, 12-foot-long moray eels, and fish that change their colors? In all, the aquarium is home to more than 8,000 fish, invertebrates, mammals, birds, reptiles and amphibians found around the world. The towering cylindrical **Giant Ocean Tank**, in the center of the aquarium, contains a re-creation of a Caribbean coral reef, chock-full of coral and sponges. Circle the 200,000-gallon saltwater tank to watch sharks, sea turtles, moray eels and hundreds of species of fish swim within inches of your face. Be sure to look for Myrtle, the nearly 90-year-old (and counting) resident green sea turtle.

Kids flock to the **Edge of the Sea** tide pool to dunk their hands in the water and grab hold of crabs, sea stars and urchins.

At the penguin colony *(ground floor)*, you'll see African penguins from South Africa and Namibia, rockhoppers from South America, and little blue penguins from Australia and New Zealand, frolicking on the rocks and slipping in and out of the chilled (and filtered!) Boston Harbor water. And everyone loves the harbor seals that play in the outdoor tank.

A cownose ray and a school of jacks, Giant Ocean Tank, New England Aquarium

© W. Chappell/New England Aquarium

FOR KIDS

IMAX – Adjacent to the aquarium, the massive, five-story-high, dome screen IMAX theater shows up-close-and-personal science and conservation-themed movies, some in 3D.

USS Constitution and Museum★★

Boston National Historical Park, Charlestown Navy Yard, Charlestown. 617-426-1812. www.ussconstitutionmuseum.org. Museum open Nov–Mar daily 10am–5pm; rest of the year daily 9am–6pm. Both closed Jan 1, Thanksgiving Day & Dec 25. Ship open Nov–Mar Thu–Sun 10am–3:50pm; rest of the year Tue–Sun 10am–5:50pm; www.history. navy.mil/ussconstitution. Water taxi from Long Wharf, or Green or Orange Lines to North Station.

Do you know how the USS *Constitution* got its nickname, "Old Ironsides"? It's said that cannonballs were seen bouncing off her oak sides during the War of 1812. Undefeated in battle, Old Ironsides was originally launched in Boston in 1797, making it the oldest commissioned warship afloat in the world. You'll learn that and much more on a tour of this famous ship. Climb aboard for a tour, led by an active-duty sailor. Around the old ship's nooks and crannies, you'll get an idea of life onboard.

At the museum, kids get an opportunity to hoist a sail, fight a (video) battle with the British, fire a cannon and play captain of a ship at a computer simulator. On-site artisans demonstrate traditional maritime crafts, like knot tying and model shipbuilding.

Tours of Fenway Park★★

4 Yawkey Way. 617-226-6666. www.boston.redox.mlb.com. Tours depart from the souvenir store across Yawkey Way year-round

USS Constitution

© vivalapenler/Fotolia.com

MUST DO

Puppet Show

Fairies and folk tales rule at the **Puppet Showplace Theatre**, a short "T" ride from Boston *(32 Station St., Brookline; 617-731-6400, ext 101; www.puppetshowplace.org; Green Line to Brookline Village T stop)*. A long time local favorite, the theater presents 50 shows per year. *Shows for all ages 3 and up. Schedule varies, check website; $12.*

Puppet Showplace Theatre

daily 10am–5pm (on the hour) or until 3½ hours before game time, whichever is earlier. $16 adults, $12 children (ages 3–15). Green Line to Kenmore T stop. Tickets available first-come first-served on the day of the tour only at the Gate D ticket booth. For information on game tickets, see For Fun.

Baseball aficionados and aspiring batters, here's your chance to go behind the scenes at the much-revered Fenway Park, the oldest field in Major League Baseball. The home of the 2013 World Series Champion Boston Red Sox hasn't changed much since the day it opened on April 20, 1912. You'll touch the famous **Green Monster** left-field wall (did you know that it's 37 feet tall?), visit the press box, get your photo taken by the dugout, and take a seat in the private club overlooking the field. The tour also includes a stroll around the field,

and a visit to the impressive Red Sox Hall of Fame—a premium, glassed-in seating area filled with memorabilia, photos and plaques honoring Red Sox Hall of Famers. Fenway was home to baseball greats Babe Ruth, Bobby Doerr, Cy Young, Ted Williams, Carlton Fisk and Carl Yastrzemski, among others.

Fenway's Features

- **The Bullpen** – The place where the pitchers warm up before and during a game. The coach uses the red phone in the bullpen to call for relief pitchers.
- **The Dugout** – Ball players sit here during the game. It's right at the level of the field.
- **The Green Monster** – This plastic-covered metal wall was colored green to be less distracting for the hitters.
- **Pesky's Pole** – The foul pole is 302 feet from home plate.

The Longest Home Run

You'll learn lots of fun tidbits on the Fenway Park tour. (Did you know that no player has ever hit a home run over the right-field roof at Fenway Park?) Before you leave the park, take a look into the right-field bleachers. The seat painted red marks the landing spot of the longest measurable home run hit inside Fenway Park. Ted Williams hit the home run on June 9, 1946, off the pitch of Fred Hutchinson of the Detroit Tigers. The ball flew 502 feet. Legend says that it crashed through the straw hat of the man sitting in the seat—section 42, row 37, seat 21.

FOR KIDS

Johnny Pesky, who played for the Red Sox from 1942 to 1954, batted balls off it or around it, for home runs.

◆ **Press Box** – News reporters sit in this glass-enclosed space to watch the game and write about it. The glass is unbreakable, so the people in the press box don't get hit by baseballs (balls hit the glass more often than you'd think).

Boston By Little Feet

Tours start in front of Faneuil Hall at the Samuel Adams statue (Congress St. side). Peak season Jul–Aug Fri 10am, Sat 1pm. Regular season May–Oct Sat 10am, Sun 1pm. Check website for other months, schedule changes and updates. 617-367-2345. www. bostonbyfoot.org. $10. Blue line to Aquarium/Faneuil Hall, Green Line to Government Center or Orange Line to State St. T stop.

This hour-long walking tour is the perfect kid-friendly introduction to Beantown. Designed for children

ages 6 through 12, the guided tour covers a major portion of the Freedom Trail *(see Historic Sites)*. Youngsters get a special explorer's map showing footprints leading to major locations on the tour. They'll even get to see the spot where Benjamin Franklin used to fly his kite.

Festival Fun for Kids

Boston is a non-stop party for kids, especially on festival and parade days. For more information about upcoming special events, call 888-733-2678 or visit www.bostonusa.com.

Duckling Day Parade

May (Mother's Day). 617-723-8144. Celebrate Mother's Day by dressing your little ones as their favorite characters from the children's classic *Make Way for Ducklings*. The parade, led by the Harvard University Band, marches through Boston Common *(bounded by Beacon, Boylston, Tremont & Park Sts.)*.

Harborfest Children's Day

Early July. 617-227-1528. www.bostonharborfest.com. Part of the city's popular Harborfest, this special day for kids features balloons, face painting, educational activities and more. It's held at City Hall Plaza *(Congress St.)* in downtown Boston.

Zoo Howl

Late October. 617-989-2000. www.franklinparkzoo.org. Costumed kids flock to the zoo for a safe day of trick or treating. Hold hands tight and get ready for the *boo!* as you navigate the haunted maze. Held at Franklin Park Zoo *(1 Franklin Park Rd., in Dorchester).*

PERFORMING ARTS

It's easy to make every night out in Boston a special night. The hard part is deciding among all the events on tap because, unfortunately, there's just no way you can be that many places all at once. One night you may rock out at one of the city's clubs, another might have you applauding after a rousing theater performance, and on the next, you could witness a life-altering jazz or classical music performance.

Boston Symphony Orchestra★★★

Symphony Hall, 301 Massachusetts Ave. 617-266-1492. www.bso.org. Green Line to Symphony T stop or Orange Line to Mass Ave. T stop. This highly-acclaimed orchestra, now led by music director Andris Nelsons, has been entertaining Boston audiences since 1881. Today the renowned Boston Symphony Orchestra (BSO) performs in the historic 2,625-seat Symphony Hall, which opened in 1900 and remains one of the world's finest performing-arts spaces. For its first 20 years, the BSO performed in the Old Boston Music Hall. (Now called the **Orpheum Theatre**, the venue hosts a wide range of musical events, from pop to rap and beyond. *www.crossroadspresents. com/Orpheum-theatre.*)

Touring Tip

If you're looking for a bargain, join the rush ticket line at Symphony Hall the day of a Boston Symphony Orchestra performance. A limited number of $9, same-day tickets are available for Tuesday and Thursday evenings and Friday afternoons and evenings *(one per customer; cash only)*. Can't make those nights? Attend an open rehearsal at $18 a ticket. *For more information, call 617-266-1200 or check online at www.bso.org.*

Generally, the BSO performs in Symphony Hall from October through April. But the music doesn't stop during the summer.

Symphony Hall, Boston Symphony Orchestra

©Stu Rosner/Boston Symphony Orchestra

PERFORMING ARTS

Here's What's Happening
You can get some idea of what's going on in the city with a read through *The Boston Globe*, *Boston Magazine* or the alternative weekly, *The Phoenix*. But for truly up-to-the-minute to-dos, visit their websites: *The Boston Globe* www.boston.com; *Boston Magazine*, www.boston magazine.com; *The Phoenix*, thephoenix.com.

It moves to the stage at **Tanglewood Music Center**, the BSO's summer home in the Berkshires. Also look to Tanglewood for performances by the Boston Pops and much more *(297 West St., Lenox; 413-637-1600)*.

Boston Pops★★

Symphony Hall, 301 Massachusetts Ave. 617-266-1492. www.bso.org. Green Line to Symphony T stop or Orange Line to Mass Ave. T stop.
In May and June, and during the Christmas holidays, Symphony Hall's outstanding acoustics reverberate with the sounds of the Boston Pops. The Pops' concerts, known as Promenade Concerts from their launch in 1885 through the 1899 season, introduced America to some of the country's most-treasured summer music

traditions: concerts with cafe-style seating and a three-part program, featuring light classical music, a soloist, and a not-necessarily classical big finish ranging from Broadway to big band to patriotic tunes.

In 1974 the orchestra kicked off a now annual duo of traditions: the Fourth of July and "Holiday Pops" Christmas holiday concerts. The Boston Pops' tradition of a week of free outdoor shows in summer, culminating in its famous Fourth of July concert (complete with eye-popping fireworks), continues at the **Hatch Shell on the Charles River Esplanade★**. Pack a great picnic, throw down a blanket and join the crowds. Get there early (and bring a book or a board game) for this highly popular event.

Boston Pops

©Stu Rosner/Boston Symphony Orchestra

Boston Center for the Arts ★★

539 Tremont St., between Berkeley & Clarendon Sts., South End. 617-426-5000. www.bcaonline.org. Green Line to Copley Square T stop or Orange Line to Back Bay T stop.

If you're looking for cutting-edge theater and art, this one-stop center in Boston's trendy **South End** *(see Neighborhoods)* is the place to go. The four-acre complex includes resident companies the Speakeasy Stage Company, Company One and the Theater Offensive, known for their contemporary — and often daring—plays and performances. Hosting more than 45 productions each year, the center is considered one of the best venues in Boston for small-theater offerings. The **Boston Ballet**, led by artistic director Mikko Nissinen, also houses its school, practice venues and administrative offices here; Boston Ballet performances are held at the Boston Opera House *(539 Washington St.; 617-695-6955; www.bostonballet.org).*

The 23,000-square-foot **Cyclorama**, an 1884 building on the National Register of Historic Places, is home to an array of changing exhibits and performances showcasing contemporary works by established and emerging artists. It also houses the Community Music Center of Boston, the Art Connection, the Boston Ballet Costume Shop, three small theaters and a rehearsal studio. Originally an organ factory built in 1850, the **Tremont Estates Building** now encompasses more than 50 artists' studios, as well as the **Mills Gallery**, where the

Touring Tip

On a budget (or just hoping to get more entertainment bang for your bucks)? Head to one of ArtsBoston's **BosTix** kiosks at Faneuil Hall *(617-262-8632; www.bostix.org; Tue–Sat 10am–6pm, Sun 11am–4pm)* or Copley Square at the corner of Boylston and Dartmouth streets *(Tue–Sat 10am–6pm, Sun 11am–4pm).* Get there early and you're likely to snag same-day, half-price tickets to some of the city's top performances of music, theater, dance and opera. Just be sure you're sure because all sales are final.

BCA stages about six large-scale exhibits a year *(open year-round Wed & Sun noon–5pm, Thu–Sat noon–9pm).* Along with the art and performances, the BCA also offers plenty of opportunities to listen in on artist and curator talks and other related events. Don't miss the annual South End Open Studios event *(late Sept),* when the Artist Studio Building throws open its doors so the public can see what artists have been up to.

American Repertory Theater

Loeb Drama Center, 64 Brattle St., Cambridge. 617-547-8300. www.americanrepertorytheater.org. Box office open Tue–Sun noon–5pm. Red Line to Harvard T stop.

This award-winning group, currently under the artistic direction of Diane Paulus, is one of the country's most acclaimed resident theater companies. Located at the Loeb Drama Center

A.R.T.'s second-stage venue, OBERON *(2 Arrow St., Cambridge)*, offers an eclectic mix of performances that push the boundaries of traditional "theater." You may find aerialists, spoken-word poets, or experimental dance troupes performing here.

on Harvard Square in Cambridge, the company presents a mix of drama, music, comedy, classics and new works.

Berklee Performance Center

136 Massachusetts Ave. 617-747-2261. www.berklee.edu/BPC. Box office open Mon–Sat 10am–6pm, and 2 hours prior to show time on performance days. Green Line to Hynes T stop.

Here's the place to hear jazz, funk, soul, gospel, Celtic, Latin and more at wallet-pleasing prices: $5 to $10 for most events. The 1,215-seat hall, part of the Berklee College of Music, is known for its 200-plus performances a year of music from around the world, as well as by the college's top talent.

Colonial Theatre

106 Boylston St. 617-426-9393. www.citicenter.org/colonial. Box office open: Tue–Sat 10am–6pm. Green Line to Boylston St. T stop or Red Line to Chinatown T stop. Tickets available online at www.boston.broadway.com.

Since the day the doors opened in 1900—*Ben-Hur* was the first show—theater-goers have been as dazzled by the Colonial's opulent interior as they have been by the shows on its stage. Present-day sponsorship contracts have renamed the venue the Citi Emerson Colonial Theatre, but the 1,700-seat space retains its historic beauty thanks to the restoration of plasterwork, intricate murals, vivid stenciling and shimmering gold leaf. Boston's oldest continuously operating theater, the Colonial today is a popular venue for pre-Broadway tryouts.

Jordan Hall at the New England Conservatory

30 Gainsborough St. 617-585-1260. www.necmusic.edu. Most concerts are free, no tickets are required. For ticketed events, box office hours: Mon–Fri 10am–6pm, Sat noon–6pm, 1.5 hours before the start of ticketed performances. Green Line E train to Symphony T stop or Orange Line to Mass Ave. T stop.

One of America's finest concert venues, Jordan Hall has nearly perfect acoustics. The historic 1,013-seat building (built in 1903) serves as the performance hall for the **New England Conservatory**, an internationally-recognized music conservatory that uses the plush hall for lectures, seminars and some 600 free classical, jazz and improvisational music concerts every year.

The hall is also home to the **Boston Philharmonic** *(617-236-0999; www.bostonphil.org)*. Conducted by Benjamin Zander, who has led the BPO since 1979, the orchestra features professional, amateur, and student musicians. Don't miss Zander's much-loved **pre-concert lectures** *(Sat at 6:45pm)*, which include his personal

Wang Theatre

© Citi Performing Arts Center/Frank C. Grace

insights into the music. The maestro quickly turns people new to classical music into devoted fans.

The BPO also performs on Sunday afternoons at the Sanders Theatre at Harvard University *(45 Quincy St., Cambridge)*. The pre-concert lecture for the Sanders Theatre Series begins at 1:45pm. *(Box office: 1350 Massachusetts Ave., Cambridge; open Tue–Sun noon–6pm; 617-496-2222; www.ofa.harvard.edu)*

Wang Theatre and Shubert Theatre at Citi Performing Arts Center
Wang Theatre: 270 Tremont St. Shubert Theatre: 265 Tremont St. 866-348-9738. www.citicenter.org. Green Line to Boylston St. T stop, Red Line to Park St. T stop or Orange Line to New England Medical T stop. Box office open Mon–Sat 10am–6pm and two hours before performances.
Home to two of Boston's historic theaters, the Citi Performing Arts Center hosts everything from hip hop shows to Broadway's biggest blockbusters.

The 3,600-seat **Wang Theatre** is a prominent landmark in Boston's historic theater district. It underwent a massive $9.8 million restoration in the early 1990s. Today the 1925 building, which looks like one of Louis XIV's palaces, glitters with chandeliers and imported marble.

Its smaller sibling, the **Shubert Theatre**, is styled like an intimate turn-of-the-19C theater (it opened in 1910). Nicknamed "The Little Princess of the Theater District," the Shubert is home to many not-for-profit performing arts organizations, including the Boston Lyric Opera *(www.blo.org)*. It also hosts touring companies throughout the year.

Once seated, be sure to take a look up at the magnificent Petit Trianon-style chandelier in the main auditorium.

PERFORMING ARTS

SHOPPING

Boston's retail scene appeals to many tastes. Thrifty Yankees, affluent international students with platinum credit cards, well-heeled Brahmins, trend setters, vintage-fashion fans and Cambridge beads-and-Birks types all have their shopping haunts. Sometimes, they even overlap; Newbury Street, for example, has everything from Cartier to comic books. Of course, this college town also offers plenty of places to pay if you're anxious to load your bookshelves with new reads or warm up in a university-logo hoodie sweatshirt.

Faneuil Hall Marketplace

©Jorge Salcedo/Fotolia.com

Faneuil Hall Marketplace★★

State St. at Congress St. 617-523-1300. www.faneuilhall marketplace.com. Open year-round Mon–Sat 10am–9pm (winter until 7pm), Sun noon–6pm. Aquarium/Faneuil Hall, Government Center or State St. T stops.

A shell's toss from Union Oyster House *(see Must Eat)*, this urban marketplace is also known as **Quincy Market**, for the long Greek Revival-style arcade that serves as the centerpiece of the complex. In total, three restored granite buildings constructed in 1825 house numerous shops, full-service restaurants and food stalls that serve up local (and international) favorites. The place is more of a draw for its ambience than its retail mix. The complex attracts hordes of tourists who might well find the same shops, like Ann Taylor and Sunglass Hut, in their own local malls. If you are after a Boston souvenir or three, buy a traditional bowl

Touring Tip

Faneuil Hall's stores may be loaded with goods a-plenty but the biggest draw is the tasty (and wide-ranging) fare sold at Quincy Market. The food stalls make for great grazing. Get your "chowdah" here, your pizza there and a gooey Boston baked brownie over yonder. Though most Bostonians would be loathe to admit it, this touristy haunt is a great place to go for Sunday brunch.

at **Boston Pewter Company**
(www.bostonpewtercompany.com), a
university-logo emblazoned t-shirt
or cap at **Boston Campus Gear**'s
kiosk, or a giant lobster stuffed
animal at **Best of Boston**.
Whether you find the perfect
purchase here or not, there's a
buzz at Faneuil Hall, created by the
presence of jugglers, musicians
and street performers. A show is
always going on (just be prepared
to be pulled in as an on-the-spot
assistant). You may even see a
Benjamin Franklin look-alike. Fun
photo op: pose a loved one next to
the bronze of a cigar-chompin' Red
Auerbach, legendary coach of the
Boston Celtics from 1950 to 1966.

Newbury Street★★

*Between Commonwealth Ave.
& Boylston Sts., Back Bay.
www.newbury-st.com. Arlington,
Copley or Boylston T stops.*
Dress the part if you plan to
stop into the designer shops on
Newbury Street—Boston's most
upscale shopping drag is the city's
answer to New York's Fifth Avenue.
A picture-perfect retail row lined
with spiffy town houses, Newbury
Street boasts a happy sprinkling of
boutiques, restaurants, ice-cream
shops and sidewalk cafes. Set
in Back Bay, the street is easy to
navigate: cross streets are lettered

from A (Arlington) to H (Hereford).
For those with grown-up tastes
and the cash to afford them,
Newbury Street offers plenty of
places to lay those Benjamins
down, including **Cartier** (no. 40),
Burberry (no. 2) and **Chanel
Boutique** (no. 6).
Labelistas will continue to kvell
over nearby Newbury Street
neighbors like **Giorgio Armani**
(no. 22), **Marc Jacobs** (no. 81) and
Kate Spade (no. 117). For a taste of
the tropics, off to **Tommy Bahama**
you go (no. 154). Want to keep some
of your cash for the rest of your
trip but still amp up your style
quotient? Make your way to **Urban
Outfitters** (no. 361) and the well-
priced shoe heaven called **Thom
Brown** (no. 331).
Don't leave Newbury without a
visit to the retail and exhibition
galleries of the 🔹 **Society of
Arts and Crafts**, America's oldest
non-profit craft organization (no.
175). The retail gallery stocks the

SHOPPING

perfect gift for every personality, thanks to an ever-changing selection of pieces by more than 200 artists from around the US.

Copley Place

100 Huntington Ave. 617-262-6600. www.simon.com. Copley T stop. Connects to Prudential Center via the skywalk.

Located behind the Boston Public Library, Copley Place is the only mall in Boston proper. And a swank one it is, with rosy marble and polished brass. High-end retailers like **Louis Vuitton, Jimmy Choo** and **Tiffany & Co.** reside here, along with anchor **Neiman Marcus**—more than 75 in all. Less familiar names are sprinkled among the biggies. Some to seek out: **Wolford**, for fine lingerie and

hosery; **Thomas Pink**, for tailored classic shirts; and **The Art of Shaving**, for grooming products that will make any man want to look after his skin.

Downtown Crossing

Intersection of Washington, Winter & Summer Sts. 617-261-0066. www.downtowncrossing. org. Downtown Crossing T stop.

This lively pedestrian mall, tucked behind Boston Common, is a colorful retail mishmash of big department stores, pushcart vendors and diamond merchants. Madly in love? Spring for some bling at one of the dozens of jewelers that call Downtown Crossing home. Madly in love with shoes? Face temptation at **DSW Shoes** and **Johnston & Murphy**, among others. Downtown Crossing is a favorite haunt of bargain hunters, too, thanks to discount stores like **H&M, Marshall's, T.J. Maxx** *(all at 350 Washington St.)* and the **Eddie Bauer Outlet** *(500 Washington St.)*.

Forgot to bring some essential clothing items with you? Make the **Macy's** department store *(450 Washington St.)* your first stop.

Downtown Crossing

The store sells a wide variety of clothing designers—high and low—and the shoe department is big enough to keep footwear fanatics busy for hours.

Outlets and Resale

The closing of the hallowed Filene's Basement in 2011 left Boston bargain-hunters bereft. But morning dawns after mourning, and with it the chance to explore sweet deals at discount, outlet and resale stores in and around Boston.

Nordstrom Rack – *497 Boylston St., Back Bay. 857-300 2300. www.shop.nordstrom.com. Mon–Thu 10am–8pm, Fri–Sat 10am–9pm, Sun 11am–6pm.* The popular high-end department store chain stocks its Rack stores with discounted merchandise from its online and brick-and-mortar sites. Two floors are stuffed with off-price designer finds, and the store is nicely organized, so treasure-hunting is unusually easy.

Second Time Around *176 Newbury St. Back Bay (other locations nearby). 617-247-3504. www.secondtimearound.net. Mon–Thu 10am–7pm, Fri–Sat 11am–8pm, Sun 11am–6pm.* The Boston locations of the national chain carry pre-owned designer items (either new or in mint condition) on a consignment basis. Prices are right up there by secondhand standards, but the quality and selection (look for Chanel, Jimmy Choo, Prada and more) can't be beat.

Haymarket

Bordering Blackstone St., just north of Faneuil Hall Marketplace. Say what you will about homogenized, one-size-fits-all American shopping, but real shopping—as in haggling, shouting, pushing and shoving—is not dead yet. Boston has the Haymarket, a colorful outdoor marketplace of fish sellers and purveyors of fresh flowers and produce. Located near Faneuil Hall Marketplace, and a hop and a skip from the North End—Boston's "Little Italy"—the Haymarket is a Friday-and-Saturday-only shopping event. Assertive vendors offer "a bagga oranges, only a dollah!" and other bargains that get better as the day progresses. Like many a good marketplace, there's no official opening or closing time, although the action generally starts around 6:30am (best time to find parking in the 'hood as well) and goes until everything is gone.

The produce is better earlier (vendors will yell at you if you pick and choose—this is strictly "grab-and-go" shopping), but the prices are cheaper later. Then again, moods worsen, so you're on your own here. Watch out for the super salesfolk—they're so skilled, you may well end up heading home

Touring Tip

"Customer service" at the Haymarket is colorful, authentic and loud, so grow a thick skin before you venture forth. Arm yourself with plenty of small bills, make your decisions quickly and above all—above all—don't touch the wares. Take a good hard look at the more perishable fruits and veggies (berries, avocados) before taking the plunge; hardier varieties may be your best bet here.

Typical souvenirs from Boston

©Chee-Onn Leong/Fotolia.com

with a bag full of eels or other impulse items.

The Shops at Prudential Center

800 Boylston St. 617-236-3100 or 800-746-7778. www.prudential center.com. Mon–Sat 10am–9pm Sun 11am–6pm. Copley T stop. Connects to Copley Place via the skywalk.

The towering 52-story "Pru" is one of Boston's best-known landmarks, combining office, residential and retail space. During Boston's interminable winters, the

Baubles and Bijoux

Keep your Tiffany's and your Cartier. Proper Bostonians tend to buy their baubles and bling bling at Shreve, Crump & Low *(39 Newbury St.; 800-225-7088; www.shrevecrumpandlow.com)*, America's oldest jewelry store. Founded in 1796, Shreve's carries a wide range of fine (if not wildly funky) jewelry, china, home decor, bridal gifts and exclusive Boston souvenirs, like the cunning, must-have swan boat brooch.

Prudential Center is a "two-fer" shopping zone, since the Pru is a short-but-labyrinthine indoor walk from Copley Place. Among the 75-plus shops and restaurants are **Saks Fifth Avenue**, **Lord & Taylor** and Boston's largest **Barnes & Noble** bookstore. Most of these stores—The Body Shop, Ann Taylor—you've seen before, but on a weathery day, you won't mind. You can even do a quick workout at the Boston Sports Club or Flywheel Sports. The Pru also offers plenty of places to fortify yourself mid-shopping, including popular eateries like **California Pizza Kitchen** and **Legal Sea Foods**.

Boutiques Around Town

Big-name stores tend to get the lion's share of shopping attention from out-of-towners. But, if you're on the hunt for one-of-a-kind finds, hit some of the city's best boutiques. From the North End to the South End (and pretty much everywhere in between) tiny specialty shops have been cropping up in recent years. Here, some best bets if you want to take home something truly special:

Salmagundi – *765 Centre St., Jamaica Plain. 617-522-5047. www.*

salmagundiboston.com. Tue–Fri noon–8pm, Sat 11am–8pm, Sun 11am–6pm.
Hats are the focus here—the shop stocks thousands of posh toppers for any occasion, many of them custom-designed. The fun-loving and helpful staff willingly takes on the task of trimming and embellishing any of the wares to create a perfect product. You'll also find interesting jewelry, handbags, silk ties and other accessories.

in-jean-ius – 441 Hanover St., North End. 617-523-5325. www.injeanius.com. Mon–Sat 11am–7pm, Sun noon–6pm.
With just one visit, you'll wipe out the need for a year's worth of exhausting shopping trips in search of the perfect pair of jeans. The name says it all. in-jean-ius offers styles by more than 30 denim designers. Prices start around $75 and go up, up and away.

Flock – 274 Shawmut Ave., South End. 617-391-0222. www.flockboston.com. Tue–Sat 11am–7pm, Sun noon–6pm.
Inspired boho-chic fashions beckon from the racks of this ultra-trendy hideaway, the brainchild of a mother-daughter team. Look no farther if you're in the market for a handcraft macramé headband studded with precious stones, the perfect hippie-themed wedding gift, or crafty Christmas ornaments and housewares.

Riccardi – 116 Newbury St., Back Bay. 617-266-3158. www.riccardi boston.com. Mon–Sat 11am–7pm.
A thoughtfully curated selection of designer apparel for men and women draws trend-hungry shoppers with deep pockets to this popular Newbury Street spot. Spendy for sure, but follow the sales staff's expert advice and you'll look like a million bucks.

Crush Boutique – 131 Charles St., Beacon Hill. 617-720-0010. www.shop crushboutique.com. Mon–Sat 10am–7pm, Sun noon–6pm.
Though the displays are fashion-forward goodies, there's nothing snobby about Crush. It's clear from the get-go that the people who work here really want their customers to have fun and head out on the town looking, well, crush-worthy.

© Gwen Cannon/Michelin

Charles Street shops

NIGHTLIFE

Grumble, grumble… yes, you'll hear some complaining about Boston's early last call (doors close, lights out at 2am). But until then, the city rocks. From funky neighborhood pubs to upscale wine bars, massive dance clubs to tiny live-music venues, you'll find plenty of sizzling nightspots to keep you entertained.

The Beehive

© The Beehive

BARS AND PUBS

The Beehive

541 Tremont St., in the Boston Center for the Arts (Cyclorama), South End. 617-423-0069. www. beehiveboston.com. Copley T stop.
With an eye toward giving Boston's artier 30-something crowd a place of their own, The Beehive opened in the former boiler room of the Cyclorama *(see Performing Arts)* in 2007. Part supper club, part art gallery, the two-floor Beehive entertains with nightly jazz shows, cabaret and burlesque

acts; some of the best late-night people meeting in the South End; an extensive cocktail menu; and the tastiest sage and sea salt frites you'll ever encounter.

Bin 26 Enoteca

26 Charles St., Beacon Hill. 617-723-5939. www.bin26.com. Charles/MGH & Arlington T stops.
Whether you're in town with a small group or traveling solo, take a seat at this wine bar's bar. When it comes to pairing customers with a soon-to-be-favorite new wine, the bartenders are great

Sing-along Fun

It's not just a piano bar, it's a dueling piano bar, with live bands turning out covers of pop songs that everyone knows the words to. If you're ready to belt 'em out with the best of 'em, make a beeline for **Howl at the Moon**, the Boston location of a well-known national chain *(184 High St.; 617-292-4695; www.howlatthemoon.com; Aquarium T stop)*. It's a hootin', hollerin' good time.

Fenway Favorites

Who's On First (19 Yawkey Way; 617-247-3353), located on the first-base side of Fenway Park, is one of the city's oldest sports bars. Expect crowds on game days; the dance club is popular with local college kids. (If you don't have a ticket to the Red Sox game, use the rear entrance on Brookline Avenue.) Need to commiserate (or celebrate) with loyal Sox fans? Head to the **Cask 'n Flagon** (62 Brookline Ave.; 617-536-4840; www.casknflagon.com), a nitty-gritty bar beyond the legendary Green Monster, or **Boston Beer Works** (61 Brookline Ave.; 617-536-2337; www.beerworks.net), with plenty of big-screen TVs and their own microbrews.

matchmakers— and with 60 wines by the glass, you're sure to find a new love.

Bukowski's Tavern
50 Dalton St., Back Bay. 617-437-9999. www.bukowskitavern.net Prudential T stop.
Pick from the "99 Bottles of Beer on the Wall" menu (there's actually more than 100 choices) or let the bartender's "Wheel of Decision" make the choice for you. This is a great happy-hour hangout, but be aware—their motto is "Great Food. Great Beer. Surly Service."

Drink
348 Congress St., Fort Point. 617-695-1806. www.drinkfort point.com. South Station T stop.
Craft cocktails are the focus at this friendly bar in the Fort Point neighborhood. It may not be the wildest party in town, but the knowledgeable mixologists more than make up for it with their artfully blended potions made with artisanal ingredients, either exquisitely sourced or made in-house. You'll also find well-curated beer and wine lists and a menu of small and large plates.

Jillian's Boston
145 Ipswich St., Kenmore Square. 617-437-0300. www.jillians boston.com. Kenmore T stop.
Located behind Fenway Park, this massive, 70,000-square-foot complex features three floors of entertainment, including an MTV spring break-esque restaurant and dance club; billiards, foosball, ping pong and beyond; and, up on the third floor, one of the snazziest bowling alleys you'll ever see.

The Living Room
101 Atlantic Ave., North End. 617-723-5101. www.theliving roomboston.com. Haymarket, Government Center or Aquarium T stops.
Round up a posse and relax on the wide couches at this homey-yet-edgy waterfront watering hole, housed within the handsome Mercantile wharf building near Faneuil Hall. Martinis win raves here, as does the inspired dance music. If you're hungry, order up a sampler of deliciously topped flatbreads, a sizzling steak, or the ultimate mac-and-cheese studded with lobster and perfumed with white truffle essence.

NIGHTLIFE

Irish Pubs

Craving colcannon and Guinness? You're in luck. Boston is packed with Irish pubs—though some are far more worth your time than others. The **Black Rose** *(160 State St.; 617-742-2286; www.blackroseboston. com)*, located steps from Faneuil Hall, is legendary for its fast-flowing Guinness and live daily Irish entertainment. Or take a seat at the Theater District's **Intermission Tavern** *(228 Tremont St.; 617-451-5997; www.intermissiontavern.com)* and discuss the play you just saw.

Lucky's Lounge
355 Congress St., Fort Point Channel. 617-357-5825. www.luckyslounge.com South Station T stop.

If Sinatra were still around, it's a sure bet that Lucky's would be his go-to place in Boston. (It even serves his favorite omelet at Sunday brunch.) The lounge/restaurant is serious about cocktails (the Lady Luck rolls down the throat just fine, thank you) as well as nightly entertainment. Just make sure you take the address with you: in true speakeasy style, there's no Lucky's sign outside.

Mr. Dooley's
77 Broad St., Downtown. 617-338-5656. Aquarium T stop.

Mr. Dooley's bartenders are masters of chatting, bantering and drawing foaming pints of Guiness, which tastes just right in this quintessential Irish neighborhood pub. The authentic Irish breakfast, complete with Boston brown bread, is a hit, as are the powerful cocktails.

Sonsie
327 Newbury St., Back Bay. 617-351-2500. www.sonsie boston.com. Hynes T stop.

Newbury Street sports a number of bars and outdoor cafes, but none is more popular than Sonsie. Sipping a starfruit martini while sitting at the restaurant's long mahogany bar has been an age-old favorite activity for Boston's beautiful people. But the bar has some serious competition now. A wine buff? Seek a table in the Wine Room on the lower level.

DANCE CLUBS

Emerald Lounge
200 Stuart St. Downtown. 617-457-2626. www.emerald ultralounge.com. Boylston or Arlington T stop.

If dressing up for a night of sweaty grooves suits your fancy, head on over to the Emerald and dance the night away. The swanky interior draws fans of hiphop, techno and electronic beats, catered to by an army of friendly bartenders.

The Estate
1 Boylston Pl., Downtown. 617-351-7000. www.theestate boston.com. Boylston T stop.

This is big thumping-music club action at its Boston best. When you're too tired to dance anymore, take a seat on one of The Estate's banquettes—you never know who you'll end up chatting with.

MUST DO

Oak Long Bar, Fairmont Copley Plaza

Looking for a Little Romance?
Some of the most romantic spots are tucked away in the dark corners of the city's elegant hotels. The opulent **Oak Long Bar at the Fairmont Copley Plaza** (138 St. James Ave.; 617-267-5300; www.fairmont.com) is among the best, with its marble bar, gilded ceilings, tall windows, dark wood paneling and plush seats. The **Bristol Lounge at the Four Seasons Hotel** (200 Boylston St.; 617-338-4400; www.fourseasons.com/boston) boasts views of the Public Garden, luscious leather couches and a cozy fireplace.

Paradise Rock Club
967 Commonwealth Ave., Boston Univ. area. 617-562-8800. www. crossroadspresents.com/ paradise-rock-club. Green line B train to Pleasant St. T stop.
It's been more than 30 years since U2 made its US debut at the Paradise, but the rock club has yet to slow down. Long a home for alternative rock bands, it showcases bands big and small.

Royale
279 Tremont St., Downtown. 617-338-7699. www.royaleboston.com. Boylston T stop.
The grand ballroom and lovely chandeliers recall the days when this place was home to the historic Wyndham Tremont Hotel. It remains a favorite with high-energy party goers who like a lot of bells, whistles and glitter with their music.

Underbar
275 Tremont St., Downtown. 617-292-0080. www.underbar online.com. Boylston T stop.
Music conoisseurs rank this spot high on their list of faves, thanks to the expert DJs, edgy atmosphere and blow-your-hair-back sound system. If you don't have a problem with heights, the Underbar's catwalk offers an alternative spot to shake your shimmy.

All that Jazz
Boston's jazz scene is small on spaces but huge on talent. Three mainstays of the jazz scene are **Ryles Jazz Club** in Cambridge (212 Hampshire St. at Inman Square; 617-876-9330; www.rylesjazz.com), Boston's premier jazz venue; the elegant **Regattabar** at the Charles Hotel (1 Bennett St.; 617-395-7757; www.regattabarjazz.com); and **Scullers** (400 Soldiers Field Rd.; 617-562-4111; www.scullersjazz.com) located in the Doubletree Suites Hotel.

NIGHTLIFE

SPAS

Are Bostonians too Puritan-practical to enjoy the pleasures of spa-dom? Not a chance! In fact, it's nearly impossible to find a spot on Newbury Street that's out of direct sight of a spa—that's how numerous they are. Given the mean streets (as in pedicure-punishing cobblestones) and harsh climate they have to deal with, Bostonians need—nay, deserve—a fair amount of pampering. At least, that's their excuse. Here's a look at the city's poshest palaces of spa goodness.

Bella Santé

38 Newbury St., Back Bay. 617-424-9930. www.bellasante.com. Arlington T stop.

Ultra-homey, with lots of candles and overstuffed couches, Bella Santé is a cocoon of healthy hedonism. It offers a full range of head-to-toe spa treatments, and all services—from massages to facials and more—are tailored to both men and women. For women anxious to fight off Father Time, book an 80-minute "Lift and Firming" facial ($240); the scent of the sunflower, clove, thyme and lemon facial massage mix alone will make you feel a decade or two younger. Call early for an appointment to have your nails done: the spa's manicures ($27 for a 30-minute manicure) are legendary.

Bliss Spa

At the W Boston hotel, 100 Stuart St., Theatre District. 617-261-8747. www.blissworld.com. Boylston T stop.

There's an energizing, upbeat atmosphere at this outpost of the popular New York-based chain. Enjoy selections from the rhythm and blues soundtrack or sample bites from the brownie bar before partaking of Bliss' renowned spa services, including body treatments, facials and massages that leave clients taut, toned, rejuvenated and happy. Make time during your visit for a steamy shower with eucalyptus oil.

Chuan Body + Soul

At The Langham hotel, Boston. 250 Franklin St., Downtown. 617-451-1900. www.chuanbody andsoul.com. State Street T stop.

You have to take a short test based on traditional Chinese medicine before you can begin your treatment. How else will the massage therapist know which essential oils to use to bring your five elemental forces back into balance? Don't worry, there are no right answers and

Bella Santé

© Bella Santé

MUST DO

instead of a gold star, you'll be rewarded with one of Boston's most soothing massages ($140 for 60 minutes). Bring your swim suit or workout gear when you visit; you can use The Langham's indoor pool and fitness facilities

Emerge Spa and Salon

275 Newbury St., Back Bay. 617-437-0006. www.emergespa salon.com. Arlington T stop.

Spend an hour or a day here and you'll indeed emerge refreshed and renewed from the wide assortment of restorative and indulgent treatments offered. In addition to herbal wraps, buffs, scrubs, facials and massages, you'll find alternative therapies such as Reiki Crystal Therapy and Craniosacral Therapy ($120 for 60 minutes) to restore balance and relieve migraines.

Gentlemen in need of pampering head for the mahogany-sleek Men's Club, with spa services and treatments including shaves, manicures, pedicures and hydrating facial treatments.

Exhale Mind Body Spa

28 Arlington St., Back Bay. 617-532-7000. www.exhalespa.com. Arlington T stop.

A welcome spot to take sanctuary amid Back Bay's hustle and bustle, Boston's Exhale, one of the flagship's 19 locations across the US, offers a variety of face and body treatments (all using organic products). But Exhale goes far beyond being just being a spa; the 12,000-square-foot facility also has an organic cafe, work-out rooms and more. Exhale's signature Core Fusion™ mind-body classes,

emphasizing core conditioning and yoga, are also available in a variety of formats.

g2o Spa + Salon

278 Newbury St., Back Bay. 617-262-2220. www.g2ospasalon.com. Hynes T stop.

After an hour or two here, you'll be sleeker, more gorgeous and a lot calmer. The whole spectrum of face and body treatments is offered, as well as unusual services such as Brine Inhalation Therapy to soothe your overtaxed respiratory system; and the Bali Paradise Experience, a combination of skin treatments amid therapeutic steam. Be sure to schedule a session in the Nap Pod, perfectly outfitted for the ultimate rest.

Grettacole Spa

At the Westin Copley Place Hotel, 10 Huntington Ave., Copley Place, Back Bay. 617-266-6166. www.grettacole.com. Copley T stop.

Conveniently located in the Westin Copley Place Hotel (there's an additional location in Wellesley), this full-service spa offers custom facials (from $100), five types of massages (including a maternity massage), body treatments, hair removal and beauty salon options. The Gretta Body Bronze ($115 including exfoliation) is a popular choice during Boston's bleak winters.

EXCURSIONS

Yet another great thing about Boston: a host of worthy day trips lie only an hour's drive or so away. Head north to Salem and Cape Ann, west to Lexington, Concord and Sturbridge, and south to New Bedford and Plymouth (home of that famous rock). You may encounter witches, colonial villagers or Minutemen among the locals. Heading east will just get you wet!

Old Sturbridge Village★★★

60mi southwest of Boston in Sturbridge. Take I-90 (Mass. Tpk.) west to Exit 9. Turn right after the tolls onto Rte. 20 West; after a half-mile, turn right. 508-347-3362 or 800-733-1830. www.osv.org. Open Apr–Oct daily 9:30am–5pm. Rest of the year, call for hours. $24 (good for 2 days within a 10-day period; ticket must be validated first visit).

If you want to escape all things modern for a day (or give your kids a lesson in what real household chores looked like), come to this living-history museum that re-creates life between 1790 and 1840 in rural New England. You'll amble in and out of some 40 buildings moved here or constructed on the 200-acre site. You can watch interpreters in 19C dress farm the land and make tools the old-fashioned way. Seasonal activities—like picking apples in the fall or shearing sheep in spring—are yours for the choosing. *At the entrance pick up a site map and a schedule of events.*

The village was initiated by Albert and Joel Cheney Wells and their

families to exhibit their collections of American antiques. Opened in 1946, the museum has grown to include historic houses, farm buildings, mills, meetinghouses, taverns and shops. Permanent exhibits display some of the museum's 50,000 artifacts such as clocks, firearms, glassware and textiles.

Old Sturbridge Village is truly a four-season delight. Visit the website for a full calendar of events. Here's a sampling:

Summer – Find out how early 19C Americans celebrated Independence Day at Village's 1830s-style July 4th event. Or, in August, get up close and personal with Revolutionary War-reenactors as they set up camp at Sturbridge for a full month.

Autumn – The focus is on fall color and agriculture in September and October; New England's trees put on their best oranges, reds and golds. In early October, Apple Days celebrates the season, with apple picking, cider-making and more.

Winter – Leave the handheld video games in the hotel room.

Touring Tip

If you have children in tow, **Kidstory** is an interactive play space featuring activities that re-create daily life and chores in an 1830s village. Children ages 6-17 can attend 2-5 day **Discovery Adventures** that engage them in activities like churning butter, designing a quilt and feeding animals.

Kids find plenty to play with and explore, including old-time cooking techniques, during the village's December-long look at Christmas traditions. Come February, help bake a cake over an open hearth to celebrate George Washington's birthday. Or in March, watch maple sugar harvesting early 19C-style.

Spring – The babies are coming! The babies are coming! See the spring lambs and other newborn animals at **Freeman Farm**. In June, Muster Day kicks off with a morning flag salute and call to muster, and continues through the day with a picnic and reenactment of a battle.

Old Sturbridge Village

© Old Sturbridge Village

EXCURSIONS

A Slice of Village Life

Freeman Farm – You'll see "farmers" plowing, milking cows, building fences and performing other farm activities.

Knight Store – This well-stocked mercantile is typical of the country store that was often the sole supplier of the farmer's needs.

Printing Office – Offices such as this one usually printed books, pamphlets and broadsides (a printed page for posting or distributing).

Tin Shop – Watch a "smithy" turn out practical wares like those used in early-19C households.

Cape Ann★★

20 to 37mi north of Boston. Take US-1 north to I-95/Rte. 128. Take Exit 45, and continue east on Rte. 128 to Gloucester. Take exit 14 or 15 for Essex, exits 15 or 16 for Manchester. Visitor information: 978-283-1601 or www.capeann vacations.com.

The "other Cape" has much to recommend it—salty sea air, fishing villages, coastal estates and rocky harbors. Though you may want to focus on spending more time in Rockport, it's worth at least paying a short visit to all four Cape Ann communities. Your first stop (and breathtaking photo op) is just 20 miles out of Boston, in Manchester-by-the-Sea, where you're sure to snap dozens of pictures of the harbor. The town is also home to Singing Beach *(see Musts for Fun)*. Continue the photo follies by driving the 32-mile road *(Rtes. 127 & 127A)* that rings the periphery of Cape Ann for stunning views of the beaches and towns—including **Gloucester★**, the oldest seaport in the nation, **Rockport★**, **Essex** and **Manchester-by-the-Sea**. Below are a couple of good places to get out and wander.

Cape Ann Museum★★

27 Pleasant St., Gloucester. 978-283-0455. www.capeann museum.org. The museum is closed for renovations and scheduled to open mid-2014.

Three levels of sunlit galleries trace the history of the maritime industries here. Don't miss the wooden ship models of Gloucester's 1892 fishing fleet or the wooden statue, *Our Lady of Good Voyage*, that used to watch over fishermen from her perch at Gloucester's Portuguese church. The museum also highlights the works of 19C and 20C artists such as Winslow Homer and Fitz Hugh Lane, who were drawn to Cape Ann's light and landscape.

Fishermen's Memorial Statue

Stacy Blvd., Rte 127, Gloucester.

Dedicated on August 23, 1925, the bronze statue sits on a base of local sea green granite. It serves as a stirring memorial to all those who have lost their lives fishing Gloucester's waters since the town was settled in 1623.

Cape Ann Lanes

53 Gloucester Ave., Gloucester. 978-283-9753. www.funbowling. com. Year-round Fri–Tue from noon; Wed & Thu from 9am; call for closing hours.

Candlepin bowling is as much of a New England tradition as lobster rolls or dropping "r"s off the ends of words. Kids love it because the balls are far smaller than traditional bowling balls.

Rockport★

Follow 127A (Thatcher Rd.) to South St. In-town parking is difficult in summer season, but a shuttle bus operates every 15min between the parking lot outside town and the town center.

This former fishing village evolved as an artists' colony in the 1920s. The red fishing shack **Motif Number 1★** is the most photographed scene in America, so they say. Wander around **Bearskin Neck★**, where old fishing sheds have been converted into shops and galleries.

Twin Lighthouses

Thacher Island, one mile off the coast of Rockport. www.thacher island.org. $5 landing fee (ages 14 and older). Boat trips mid-Jun–early Sept Wed 9am & 9:45am; Sat 8am, 8:45am, 9:30am, 10:15am, 11am. Reservations required: 617-599-2590.

The 50-acre **Thacher Island** is home to the only operating twin lighthouses in the country—they're

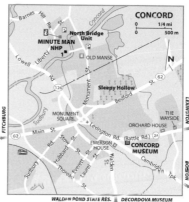

also the last lighthouses that were constructed under British rule. Space on the boat trips out to the island is limited so reserve early. Or, if you would rather go on your own power, you can kayak to the island. Once on Thacher, you can visit the lighthouses as well as other historic buildings on the island, and hike along the trails.

Concord and Lexington★★

Lexington and Concord have been linked in the minds of Americans since April 19, 1775, the day British and colonial troops clashed here, triggering the American Revolution. At the Revolutionary War sites preserved in these two neighboring cities, you can retrace the incidents that occurred on that day.

In the 19C, Concord was home to writers Ralph Waldo Emerson and Henry David Thoreau, who wrote his most famous book, *Walden*, while living at nearby Walden Pond from 1845–1847.

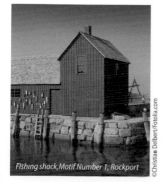

Fishing shack, Motif Number 1, Rockport

©Christian Delbert/Fotolia.com

EXCURSIONS

105

Concord★★

17mi west of Boston. Take Memorial Drive west through Cambridge, where it becomes US-3/ Rte. 2. Continue west on Rte. 2 (Concord Tpk.) to Rte. 126/Walden St. in Concord. Visitor information: 978-369-3120 or www.concord chamberofcommerce.org.

Concord Museum★ – *200 Lexington Rd., Concord. 978-369-9763. www.concordmuseum.org. Open Jan–Mar Mon–Sat 11am–4pm, Sun 1pm–4pm; Apr–Dec Mon–Sat 9am–5pm, Sun noon–5pm (Jun–Aug Sun 9am–5pm). Closed major holidays. $10.* The artifacts, documents and period rooms here give you a sense of Concord's rich history. You'll see a lantern hung in the steeple of Old North Church *(see Landmarks)* to signal Paul Revere, and objects used by Thoreau at Walden Pond *(opposite)*.

Minute Man National Historical Park★ – *Visitor Center 270 N. Great Rd., Lincoln. 978-369-6993. www.nps.gov/ mima.* This park commemorates the events that took place on April 19, 1775, along Battle Road *(Rte. 2A between Lexington and Concord)* and in Lexington, Lincoln and Concord. Take the interpretive trail that runs alongside Battle Road to learn about the Patriots' attacks on British troops retreating to Bunker Hill.

North Bridge Unit★★

A replica of the **Old North Bridge★** marks the place where colonial farmers advanced on the British and fired the "shot heard 'round the world." Emerson immortalized it in his poem *Concord Hymn*. Daniel Chester French's statue of the Minute Man *(see 1 on map p 105)* honors the Patriots who resisted the British at Concord.

Sleepy Hollow Cemetery – *Bedford St. at Partridge Lane. From Concord center, turn right onto Rte. 62. Enter the cemetery through the second gate on the left and follow signs for Authors Ridge. 978-318-3233. Open year-round daily 7am–dusk.* A short climb from the parking lot leads to the graves of the Alcotts, Nathaniel Hawthorne, Ralph Waldo Emerson, Henry David Thoreau, and others.

Walden Pond Reservation – *1.5mi south of Concord center on Rte. 126 (Walden St.).* Henry David Thoreau built his cabin on the shore of this lake. To reach the cabin site (marked by a pile of stones) from the parking lot, follow the trail signs to a granite post, where the trail turns right *(a 15-minute walk)*.

Old North Bridge

Greater Boston CVB/FayFoto, Inc.

MUST SEE

Lexington★★

7.5mi east of Concord on Rte. 2A. Visitor information: 781-862-2480 or www.lexingtonchamber.org. Visitor center located at 1875 Massachusetts Ave.; open year-round daily 9am–5pm.

Lexington Green★★ – The first confrontation between the British soldiers and the Minutemen on April 19 took place in this triangular park. Henry Kitson's statue **The Minuteman** represents the leader of the Lexington militia, Captain Parker. Seven of the colonists killed here that day are buried beneath the Revolutionary Monument.

Buckman Tavern★ – *1 Bedford St. 781-862-1703. www.lexington history.org. Visit by 30min guided tour only, but currently closed for renovation.* The Minutemen gathered here on April 18 to await the arrival of British troops.

Minute Man Visitor Center – *270 N. Great Rd. 978-369-6993. www.nps.gov/mima. Open Apr–Oct daily 9am–5pm. Rest of the year daily 9am–4pm. Closed Thanksgiving.* Exhibits and a state-of-the-art multimedia presentation entitled *The Road to Revolution (25min)* trace the events of April 19, 1775.

Plymouth★★

41mi southeast of Boston. Take I-93 south from Boston to Rte. 3. Take exit 6A into Plymouth. Visitor Center at 130 Water St. 508-747-7533 or 800-872-1620. www. seeplymouth.com. Open Jul–Aug daily 8am–8pm. Sept–Nov & Apr–Jun daily 9am–5pm.

This attractive town, with hilly streets sloping down to the harbor, is the site of the first permanent settlement in New England. The long voyage of the *Mayflower*,

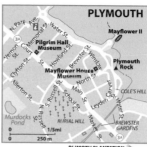

PLYMOUTH

PLIMOTH PLANTATION

the hardships that the Pilgrims endured and the eventual success of Plymouth Colony form part of the cherished story related in Plymouth's historic monuments and sites.

Plimoth Plantation★★

3mi south on Rte. 3 from the center of Plymouth; take Exit 4. 508-746-1622. www.plimoth.org. Open mid-Mar–late Nov daily 9am–5pm. $25.95 (or buy a combo pass, $29.95, good for 2 consecutive days at the Plantation and Mayflower II).

Why is it spelled "Plimoth" at this reproduction of the Pilgrims' 1627 village? The museum curators adopted this spelling from colonial Governor William Bradford's early journals.

Highlights here include **The Dwellings**, rows of thatched-roof cottages similar to those inhabited by the Alden, Carver, Bradford, Standish and other families; the **Hobbamock's Wampanoag Indian Homesite**, where staff members interpret the culture of the Wampanoag people; and the **Carriage House Crafts Center**, where workers use 17C methods to make handicrafts.

EXCURSIONS

Plimoth Plantation

Courtesy of Plimoth Plantation/ Ted Curtin

Mayflower II★★
Berthed at the State Pier. 508-746-1622. www.plimoth.org. Open mid-Mar–late Nov daily 9am–5pm. $10.
The *Mayflower II*, built in England in 1957, is a full-scale replica of the ship that carried the Pilgrims to Plymouth in 1620. You can tour the passenger quarters, see the place where the food was stored, and get a real sense of how tight the space was on the voyage.

Mayflower House Museum★
4 Winslow St. 508-746-2590. www.themayflowersociety.com. Visit by 40min guided tour only, May–Nov; call for tour days & hours and admission fee. Closed major holidays.
Not far from Plymouth Rock, this lovely mansion, set in spacious grounds, was built in 1754 by a descendant of the Pilgrim Edward Winslow. It now serves as a museum of the General Society of Mayflower Descendants, founded in 1897. The building was enlarged in the 19C and acquired by the society in 1941.
Note the broad, columned veranda, and the roof crowned with a widow's walk and cupola.
Among the antiques inside the museum are a rare set of biblical fireplace tiles in the drawing room.

Mayflower II

©PhotoDisc

Pilgrim Hall Museum★

75 Court St. 508-746-1620.
www.pilgrimhallmuseum.org.
Open Feb–Dec daily 9:30am–
4:30pm. Closed Dec 25. $8.
Built as a memorial to the Pilgrims,
this austere 1824 structure contains
original Pilgrim furnishings and
artifacts, including the cradle
of Peregine White, who was born on
the *Mayflower*.

Plymouth Rock★

On the beach at Water St.
It's not what you expect to see—
the famous boulder enclosed in a
columned structure at the water's
edge. Since it's regarded as the
stepping stone used by the *Mayflower*
passengers when they disembarked
at Plymouth, the treasured rock
must be protected for posterity!

Salem★★

15mi northeast of Boston.
Take I-93 N to I-95 N. Follow it
to Rte. 128 N. Take exit 25A and
follow Rt.e 114-E into Salem.
Visitor information: 877-725-
3662 or www.salem.org.
Say the name Salem, and witchcraft
springs to mind. The seaside city
capitalizes on its history as a 17C
town tormented by fear of witches.
Several points of interest re-create

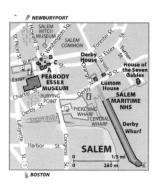

the witch-hunts, and some shops
sell witchcraft items. At Halloween
the city hosts a 10-day festival
called **Haunted Happenings**.
Visitors come to Salem for its
maritime heritage as well. After
all, it was once a bustling seaport
that launched 1,000 ships. Use the
Freedom Trail-like red line around
town to get a free tour of the top
attractions.

Peabody Essex Museum★★★

161 Essex St. 866-745-1876.
www.pem.org. Open year-round
daily 10am–5pm. Closed Jan 1,
Thanksgiving Day & Dec 25. $18.
Additional charge for Yin Yu Tang:
A Chinese House.
This illustrious museum just keeps
getting better. From its beginnings
in 1799 as the Salem East India

Witchcraft Hysteria

In 1692 several young girls, their imaginations stirred by tales of voodoo
told to them by the West Indian slave Tituba, began to have visions and
convulsive fits. After examining the girls, a doctor declared them to be
victims of "the evil hand." The frightened girls accused Tituba and two
other women of having bewitched them; the women were arrested and
jailed. In the frenzy of fear that followed, more than 200 persons were
accused of witchcraft; 150 were imprisoned and 19 found guilty and
hanged. The hysteria, credited in retrospect to rivalries between several
prominent Salem families, came to an abrupt end a year later when
Governor William Phips' wife was accused of witchcraft.

EXCURSIONS

109

Peabody Essex Museum

© Timothy Hursley/Peabody Essex Museum

Marine Society's meeting hall to the present facility, with a striking wing added in 2003, the Peabody Essex Museum has become one of the largest museums on the East Coast. Collections focus on America's maritime history from the 17C to the present, and on Salem's past, including the city's heady days in the 18C and 19C, when ship captains returned with porcelain, carvings and other treasures from the Far East, India, Africa and the Pacific Islands.

The museum has one of the most complete collections of Asian export art in the world, and counts historic houses and an extensive research library as part of its complex.

Peabody Highlights

American Decorative Arts – Furnishings, paintings, textiles, toys and costumes from the colonial period through the early 20C make up this impressive collection.

Asian Export Art – Fine examples of 19C and early-20C porcelain, silver, furniture and textiles created in China, Japan, India, the Philippines and Ceylon (now Sri Lanka) are exhibited.

Asian, African and Pacific Islands Art – Textiles, shields, ritual costumes, masks and pottery from the tropical Pacific Islands, Indonesia, Japan and Africa fill this gallery, along with 19C Meiji costumes from Japan.

Maritime Art and History – Here you'll find paintings by Fitz Hugh Lane, John Singleton Copley and Gilbert Stuart; ships' portraits commissioned by the vessels' owners; and rare nautical instruments and carved ships' figureheads.

Native American Arts and Archaeology – Artifacts here come from the Indian cultures of the Eastern seaboard, Great Lakes, Great Plains, Northwest Coast and South America.

🚶 **Yin Yu Tang –** Walk through a late Qing dynasty house that

Touring Tip

Several historic houses worth a tour, including the following, are located near the museum (entry fee included in museum admission):
Gardner-Pingree House★★ [A], a handsome brick mansion built in 1805; **John Ward House★ [B]** (1684), an example of 17C American Colonial architecture; and **Crowninshield-Bentley House [C]**, a 1730 dwelling typical of mid-18C New England architecture. The remarkable **Yin Yu Tang**, a traditional early-19C Chinese merchant's house, was relocated here, with its original furnishings, from southeast China. [A], [B] and [C] refer to the map on the previous page.

MUST SEE

New Bedford Whaling Museum★★

The museum's collections of artifacts, prints, log books and journals are among the world's finest. Paintings, scrimshaw, sailor's Valentines and more illustrate the history of whaling. *60mi south of Boston in New Bedford. I-93 south from Boston to Exit 4/21. South on Rte. 24 to Exit 12; continue south on Rte. 140 to New Bedford. To reach the museum, take I-195 east to Rte. 18; drive south to downtown exit. 18 Johnny Cake Hill. 508-997-0046. www. whalingmuseum.org. Open Apr–Oct daily 9am–5pm; Nov–Mar Tue–Sat 9am–4pm, Sun 11am–4pm. Closed Jan 1, Thanksgiving Day & Dec 25. $14.*

was moved to the Peabody from southeastern China. *See Touring Tip.*

House of the Seven Gables★
115 Derby St. 978-744-0991. www.7gables.org. Visit by 45min guided tour only, late Jun–Oct daily 10am–7pm. Rest of the year daily 10am–5pm. Closed early Jan, Thanksgiving Day & Dec 25. $12.50.

A leading 19C American literary figure, **Nathaniel Hawthorne** (1804–1864) was born in Salem, which provided the setting for many of his works. Hawthorne's novel of the same name immortalized this rambling three-story Colonial house with its steeply pitched roofs. Built in 1668, it was completely restored

in 1968. Tours include the author's birthplace.

Salem Maritime National Historic Site★
193 Derby St. 978-740 1650. www.nps.gov/sama. Open year-round daily 9am–5pm. Closed Jan 1, Thanksgiving Day & Dec 25.

Visit the city's historic waterfront to relive Salem's glory days. Of the 40 wharves that once reached out into the harbor, **Derby Wharf**, the longest (2,100 feet), remains. Guided tours *(Thu–Mon; free, but must be reserved in advance)* of the site include the **Custom House★**, where Nathaniel Hawthorne worked as a port officer; the **Derby House** (1762); and a replica of the merchant vessel *Friendship*.

©PhotoD sc

House of the Seven Gables

EXCURSIONS

CAPE COD★★★

With just one visit to Cape Cod, you'll join the legions of fans who understand that it's not just a place, but a state of mind. With so much variety on tap, finding your perfect spot on the Cape comes easy.

Curling around Cape Cod Bay like a muscular arm in flex, this oddly shaped peninsula juts out into the Atlantic Ocean some 58 miles southeast of Boston. At its fringes, you'll find 300 miles of sandy beaches, fishing villages, salt marshes and dunes covered with sea grass. You might wait several hours to cross the Sagamore Bridge onto the Cape, but once there, you won't be disappointed. And there's a Cape Cod for every personality; 15 different towns pepper the peninsula. During the summer, the bustling towns of **Hyannis** and **Provincetown★★**

Touring Tip

If you'd like a handmade souvenir, be on the lookout for the many roadside shops on the Cape, where you can purchase candles, wooden decoys, pottery, glassware and leather goods made by local artisans.

sizzle with energy. If you prefer more peaceful pleasures, they're here too—tucked down the back roads of **Falmouth★**, atop one of the striking cliffs in **Truro** or along spectacular beaches at **Cape Cod National Seashore★★★**.

MUST SEE

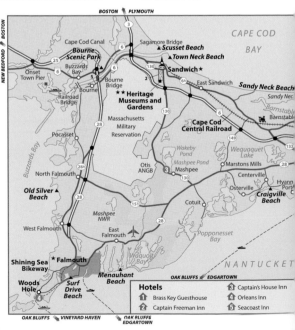

BOSTON · PLYMOUTH

CAPE COD BAY

Cape Cod Canal
Bourne Scenic Park
Sagamore Bridge
Susset Beach
Town Neck Beach
Onset Town Pier
Buzzards Bay
Bourne Bridge
Sandwich★
East Sandwich
Sandy Neck Beach
Sandy Nec
Railroad Bridge
Bourne
★★Heritage Museums and Gardens
Barnstabl
Barnstabl
Pocasset
Massachusetts Military Reservation
Cape Cod Central Railroad
Wakeby Pond
Wequaquet Lake
North Falmouth
Otis ANGB
Mashpee Pond
Mashpee
Marstons Mills
Centerville
Old Silver Beach
Cotuit
Osterville
Hyann Port
Craigville Beach
West Falmouth
Mashpee NWR
East Falmouth
Popponesset Bay
NANTUCKET
Shining Sea Bikeway
★Falmouth
Menauhant Beach
Waquoit Bay
OAK BLUFFS · EDGARTOWN
Woods Hole
Surf Drive Beach

Hotels	
1 Brass Key Guesthouse	3 Captain's House Inn
2 Captain Freeman Inn	4 Orleans Inn
	5 Seacoast Inn

OAK BLUFFS · VINEYARD HAVEN
OAK BLUFFS · EDGARTOWN

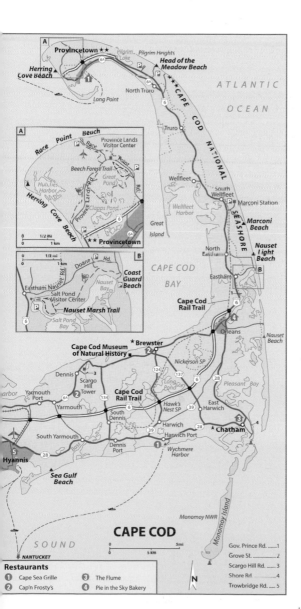

Provincetown ★★

Herring Cove Beach

Pilgrim Lake
Pilgrim Heights
Head of the Meadow Beach

ATLANTIC
OCEAN

North Truro

Long Point

Truro

CAPE COD NATIONAL SEASHORE

A
Race Point Beach
Province Lands Visitor Center
Beech Forest Trail
Race Point Rd.
Great Pond
Hatches Harbor
Herring Cove Beach
Province Lands Rd.
Clapps Pond
1957
★★ Provincetown
0   1/2 mi
0   1 km

Wellfleet
South Wellfleet
Marconi Station
Marconi Beach
Nauset Light Beach
Wellfleet Harbor

Great Island

B
Doane Rd.
Coast Guard Beach
Nauset Bay
Eastham Nauset
Salt Pond Visitor Center
Nauset Marsh Trail
Salt Pond Bay
0   1/2 mi
0   1 km

North Eastham

CAPE COD BAY

Eastham

Cape Cod Rail Trail

Orleans
Nauset Beach

Cape Cod Museum of Natural History
★ Brewster
Nickerson SP

Dennis
Scargo Hill Tower
Cape Cod Rail Trail
Long Pond
Pleasant Bay

Yarmouth Port
Yarmouth
South Dennis
Hawk's Nest SP
East Harwich

harbor
South Yarmouth
Harwich
Harwich Port
Chatham

Hyannis
Dennis Port
Wychmere Harbor

Sea Gulf Beach

Monomoy NWR

Monomoy Island

CAPE COD

SOUND

0   5mi
0   5 km

NANTUCKET

N

Restaurants	
① Cape Sea Grille	③ The Flume
② Cap'n Frosty's	④ Pie in the Sky Bakery

Gov. Prince Rd. 1
Grove St. 2
Scargo Hill Rd. 3
Shore Rd 4
Trowbridge Rd. 5

What's Where on the Cape

The Cape is divided into four areas: Upper (Sandwich, Falmouth, and Bourne), Mid (Barnstable/Hyannis, Yarmouth and Dennis), Lower (Brewster, Harwich, Chatham and Orleans) and Outer (Eastham, Wellfleet, Truro and Provincetown).

GETTING TO THE CAPE

While Cape Cod sits a teasingly-easy 75 miles from Boston's Logan Airport, a high-season drive to the Cape can take, to put it mildly, hours. Instead, consider traveling by boat, plane or bus. You can rent a car once you get there or, if you really want the full Cape Cod experience, bring or rent a bike to do your toodling around.

Bus Service – Year-round shuttle service between Logan, Plymouth and Provincetown is provided by Plymouth & Brockton Street Railway Co. (*8 Industrial Park Rd., Plymouth; 508-746-0378; http://p-b.com*). Peter Pan Bus Lines also offers bus service from Boston to points on the Cape (*800-343-9999; http://peterpanbus.com*).

Ferry Service – Bay State Cruise Co. runs boats between Boston and Provincetown (*Jul, Saturday only, 3 hours, $46 round-trip*) and high-speed ferry (*mid-May–mid-Oct daily, 1.5 hours, $88 round-trip*). Reservations suggested (*617-748-1428; for high-speed ferry 877-783-3779; www.baystatecruisecompany.com*). To sail through the *how should we get there?* process with ease, visit the Cape Cod Chamber of Commerce's travel planning website (*www.smartguide.org*). For more help, contact the Chamber directly (*5 Patti Page Way, Centerville; 508-362-3225; www.capecodchamber.org*).

UPPER CAPE

Sandwich★

The first settlement on Cape Cod, founded way back in 1637, Sandwich has long been famous for the manufacture of glass. To see glass from the 19C that was made here—as well as glass made right in front of your eyes—visit the **Sandwich Glass Museum★** (*129 Main St.; 508-888-0251; www.sandwichglassmuseum.org; open Apr–Dec daily 9:30am –5pm; Feb–Mar Wed–Sun 9:30am–4pm; closed Jan, and major holidays; $8*). And don't miss seeing the 100-acre **Heritage Museums and Gardens★★** (*Rte. 6A at Grove & Pine Sts.; 508-888-3300; http://heritagemuseumsandgardens. org; open Apr–Oct daily 10am–4pm, until 5pm late-May–early Sept; $18*), comprising an automobile museum, a military museum, an art museum, an operating hand-carved carousel and a windmill built in 1800. Known for their Dexter

Tulip Vases c. 1870, Sandwich Glass Museum Collection

Sandwich Glass Museum

Touring Tip

Part of the fun on Cape Cod is a stop at a general store, a common roadside sight throughout New England. Enter the **Brewster Store** *(1935 Main St.; 508-896-3744; www.brewsterstore.com)* and you step into a world of Americana, past and present. Get your beach and picnic supplies here, and about anything else you need. Oh, and an ice-cream cone too.

...and another Touring Tip

If you have teens or preteens in your group, they'll enjoy the scene at popular **Craigville Beach** in Centerville, with its gentle surf and warm water. MTV crews have filmed here in the past. Need we say more?

Rhododendrons, the gardens abound in the vibrant colors of seasonal blooms. Off-season, the Heritage Museums run occasional programing; call for details.

Woods Hole

At the southwest tip of the Upper Cape, two miles beyond lovely **Falmouth★**, lies the former whaling port of Woods Hole. The **Shining Sea Bikeway** links the two towns *(for details, contact the town of Falmouth; 508-548-7611; www.falmouthmass.us)*. Today Woods Hole is a world-renowned center for the study of marine life. Two private laboratories, two federal marine facilities and a science aquarium are located here, as well as the largest independent marine-research lab in the US, **Woods Hole Oceanographic Institution** *(508-289-2252; www. whoi.edu; 1hr tours Jul & Aug Mon–Fri 10:30am & 1:30pm; reservations required)*. The small town is also the departure point for ferries to **Martha's Vineyard★★** *(see p 120)*.

Upper Cape Beaches

Need a place to set up your beach chair? **Scusset Beach**, though not actually on the Cape itself, occupies a pleasant stretch of sand on the Cape Cod Canal; also on the Canal, **Bourne Scenic Park** boasts 70 acres for hiking, fishing and lake swimming. **Town Neck Beach**, on the bayside in Sandwich, offers pretty views and good swimming.

MID CAPE

Hyannis

Not ready to relax on the beach? You'll find plenty to do in this South Shore town. The largest of Barnstable's seven towns, it's the major shopping center for the Cape and the hub of airline and ferry services. There are plenty of souvenir shops and places to eat. **Cooke's Seafood** is a long-time local favorite—the fried clam platter is a must *(1120 Rte. 132; 508-775-0450; wwwcookesseafood.com)*.

Cape Cod Baseball League

Get the small town experience but see (almost) big league talent. This baseball league is loaded with some of the best collegiate players in the country *(www.capecodbaseball.org; season runs Jun–Aug)*.

CAPE COD AND THE ISLANDS

Then, at the Hyannis Depot, board a 1920s parlor car for a two-hour scenic tour offered by the **Cape Cod Central Railroad** *(252 Main St.; 888-797-7245; www.capetrain.com)*, with stops at Sandwich and the Cape Cod Canal. Or, to make an elegant evening out of it, ride the railroad's three-hour dinner train *($79 per person, includes a five-course meal)*.

Mid-Cape Beaches

Sandy Neck Beach *(Sandy Neck Rd., in Barnstable)* is considered one of the best public beaches on the Cape. The shallow pools formed here at low tide delight children. Surrounded by dunes and salt marshes, Sandy Neck has great views, to boot. On Nantucket Sound, **Seagull Beach** *(off South St., in Yarmouth; open 8am–10pm)* is another winner; calm waters here make for great swimming. It's the largest beach in Yarmouth.

LOWER CAPE

Brewster★

A charmer on the North Shore, the resort town of Brewster was first settled in the mid-17C. Many of the stately residences you'll see were built by prosperous sea captains in the 19C. Be sure to visit the **Cape Cod Museum of Natural History**

Where the Wild Things Are

One of the best things to do on the Cape? Jump on a whale-watching cruise to Stellwagen Bank, a popular feeding ground for whales; several P-town outfitters offer trips throughout the summer. Come winter, dress warmly and board a boat for a seal-watching trip offered by the Massachusetts Audubon Society's Wellfleet Bay Wildlife Sanctuary *(291 State Hwy., Rte. 6, South Wellfleet; 508-349-2615; www.massaudubon.org)*.

(869 Main St.; 508-896-3867; www.ccmnh.org; call or see website for hours; closed major holidays; $10), where you'll find interactive exhibits on the plants, animals and geology of the Cape. Take one of the three nature trails on the property *(grounds open year-round daily)* to explore salt marshes and cranberry bogs.

Once your appetite rolls in, contemplate life as an 1800s sea captain over a dinner of the day's catch at **Brewster Fish House** *(2208 Main St.; 508-896-7867; www.brewsterfishhouse.com)*. Or, in nearby Dennis, place your order at the Sesuit Harbor Cafe counter (lobster roll or fried scallops) before you head outside to make one of the waterside picnic tables your very

Touring Tip

Cape Cod Rail Trail follows a paved former rail bed 19.6 miles from South Dennis to the Salt Pond Visitor Center in Eastham, or 25.8 miles to South Wellfleet *(contact Nickerson State Park 508-896-3491 or www.mass.gov)*. **Nauset Marsh Trail** winds 1.6 miles from the Salt Pond Visitor Center through marshland to Coast Guard Beach. The staff at Cape Cod National Seashore *(opposite)* can provide details.

own *(357 Sesuit Neck Rd.; 508-385-6134; www.sesuitharbor-cafe.com)*.

Chatham★

It's easy to see why Chatham, which sits right in the bend of Cape Cod's elbow, was named a 2007 "Distinctive Destination" by the National Trust for Historic Preservation; it's pure Americana. Visit the **Caleb Nickerson House** *(1107 Orleans Rd.; 508-945-6086; www.nickersonassoc.org; tours Jun–Sept Wed 9am -1pm; $4)* built in 1772 by a Revolutionary War veteran and his wife. In 2003 the home was moved to its present location from its original spot overlooking the Oyster River. Or take a turn around the **Chatham Railroad Museum** *(153 Depot Rd.; 508-945-5100; www.chathamrailroadmuseum.com; open mid-Jun–mid-Sept Tue–Sat 10am–4pm)* inside the restored 1887 railroad depot. Highlights include a *kids will love it!* caboose.

Orleans

Orleans is the first town on the Cape where you will see ocean beaches. **Nauset Beach**, about 10 miles long, protects the surrounding towns from violent storms called nor'easters.

OUTER CAPE

Cape Cod National Seashore★★★

See map p113. In 1961, the eastern coast of the Cape, with its fragile dunes, cliffs, marshes and woodlands, became a federally protected national seashore. Choose from several beaches here (lifeguards are on duty late Jun–Aug): **Coast Guard Beach**, **Nauset Light Beach**, **Marconi Beach**, **Head of the Meadow Beach**, **Race Point Beach** and **Herring Cove Beach**. A visitor center is located at each end of the 27,000 acre seashore. Stretch your legs on the one-mile **Nauset March Trail.** *For parking passes and details, call 508-255-3421 or visit www.nps.gov/caco.*

Provincetown★★

The site of the Pilgrims' first landing, in November 1620, bustling Ptown (as regulars call it) is today one happening place. It's chock-full of art galleries, shops, dance clubs, bars, restaurants, a theater company —and tons of seasonal visitors. During the summer months, the population swells from the year-round figure of 3,400 to an incredible 75,000. A big part of the crowd comes from Ptown's long-time standing as a favorite summertime destination of gay men and women. Surrounded on three sides by beaches on the northern tip of Cape Cod *(see Cape Cod National Seashore)*, the town abounds with opportunities like

©Jerry Callaghan/iStockphoto.com
Nauset Beach

kayaking, biking, hiking, sailing and windsurfing.

For a challenging (but spectacular) bike ride, head out on the 7-mile **Province Land Trail** *(for details, visit www.nps.gov/caco).*

Then get a good look at some great art by strolling in and out of the galleries along Commercial Street, Ptown's main thoroughfare.

Pilgrim Monument & Provincetown Museum★ – *High Pole Hill Rd. 508-487-1310. www. pilgrim-monument.org. Open Apr–Nov daily 9am–5pm (late May–early Sept until 7pm). Closed Thanksgiving Day.* $12. You can't miss this granite tower, built to commemorate the Pilgrims' 1620 landing here. It rises 252 feet above the town. Climb the 166 steps, and you'll be rewarded with sweeping views of Ptown, its harbor and the lower Cape. Enter the tower through the small museum, where you'll see a model of the *Mayflower.*

Nantucket★★★

28mi south of Hyannis. Access by ferry (see sidebar) or plane. Visitor information: Nantucket Island Chamber of Commerce, 48 Main St., Nantucket; 508-228-1700; www.nantucketchamber.org.

In the Algonquian language, Nantucket means "far-away land," but this island, once the premier summer resort destination on the East Coast, lies a mere 28 miles off the Cape. Step off the ferry into the almost perfectly preserved **Nantucket village★★★**, a 19C enclave of cobblestone streets and redbrick mansions. From 1740 to the 1830s, Nantucket reigned as the world's foremost whaling port. Merchants and ship owners who grew rich selling precious whale oil built the magnificent houses lining **Main Street★★★** near the wharves. Elegant sea captains' homes now house fine restaurants, boutiques and inns.

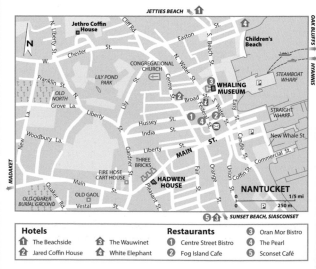

Hotels		Restaurants	
🏠 The Beachside	🏠 The Wauwinet	① Centre Street Bistro	③ Oran Mor Bistro
🏠 Jared Coffin House	🏠 White Elephant	② Fog Island Cafe	④ The Pearl
			⑤ Sconset Café

Nantucket

©Luan Tran/iStockphoto.com

Historic Sites

Don't even consider skipping the combo ticket. The **Nantucket Historical Association** (15 Broad St.; 508-228-1894; www.nha.org) all-access pass ($20) includes admission to several historic sites (open late May–mid-Oct daily 11am–4pm, call for off-season hours) and the Whaling Museum (open late May–Oct daily 10am–5pm; call for off-season hours). It's your opportunity to understand Nantucket's place in history.

For a more in-depth look at the area, take a guided walking tour ($10; departs from Whaling Museum). Sites include the **Hadwen House★** (96 Main St.), built in 1845 for a whale-oil merchant; and the **Oldest House**, also known as the

Touring Tip

Nantucket's **Black-Eyed Susan's** serves great breakfasts. Sourdough French toast (spread thick with orange Jack Daniels Butter) or the hearty Portuguese scramble with grits are reason enough to get up in the morning. But, the dishes may also send you straight back to bed for a nap. 10 India St. 508-325-0308. www.black-eyedsusans.com. Closed Sun. Breakfast and dinner only.

Jethro Coffin House (16 Sunset Hill), one of the few remaining structures from the 17C English settlement.

To Nantucket by Boat

The ferries of the **Steamship Authority** (508-477-8600; www.steamship authority.com) carry cars, passengers, pets and bikes year-round from Hyannis to Nantucket, a 2-hour-and-15-minute trip, or 1 hour by high-speed ferry (no cars or pets; reservations: 508-495-3278). **Hy-Line Cruises** offers seasonal 2-hour service and year-round 1-hour high-speed catamaran service from Hyannis; no cars allowed (800-492-8082; http://hylinecruises. com). **Freedom Cruise Line** (508-432-8999; http://nantucketislandferry. com) carries passengers and bikes, and departs from Harwich late May–late Sept daily. Whichever line you choose, keep your camera handy—it's a beautiful trip.

CAPE COD AND THE ISLANDS

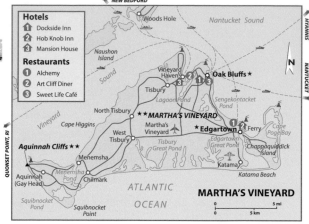

Hotels
1. Dockside Inn
2. Hob Knob Inn
3. Mansion House

Restaurants
1. Alchemy
2. Art Cliff Diner
3. Sweet Life Café

Woods Hole
Nantucket Sound
Naushon Island
Vineyard Haven
Oak Bluffs ★
Tisbury
Lagoon Pond
Sengekontacket Pond
North Tisbury
★★ MARTHA'S VINEYARD
Vineyard
Cape Higgins
Martha's Vineyard
★ Edgartown
Ferry
Cape Poge Bay
West Tisbury
Edgartown Great Pond
Chappaquiddick Island
Aquinnah Cliffs ★★
Menemsha
Tisbury Great Pond
Katama
Menemsha Pond
Aquinnah (Gay Head)
Chilmark
ATLANTIC OCEAN
Katama Beach
Squibnocket Pond
Squibnocket Point
MARTHA'S VINEYARD

QUONSET POINT, RI
HYANNIS
NANTUCKET

0   5 mi
0   5 km

The **Whaling Museum**★ *(13 Broad St.)* contains wonderful collections of scrimshaw, harpoons, ships models and an impressive skeleton of a 46-foot sperm whale. Step inside the re-created blacksmith shop, sail loft, and cooper's shop to see trades and crafts relating to the whaling industry.

Nantucket Beaches
Jetties Beach and **Children's Beach**, both on the north shore, are ideal for kids. The water stays fairly calm and kid-friendly. Jetties Beach has changing rooms, showers, a snack bar and boat rentals; Children's Beach features a playground and a picnic area. The water gets rougher on the south shore, attracting surfers. The south shore's **Surfside Beach** is popular with beachcombers, kite-flyers and surfcasters. **Madaket Beach**, at the island's west end, gets pounded by heavy surf, but the sunsets there are spectacular. No matter where you spend your sunbathing hours, head over to

Madaket, a picnic basket in hand, for nature's grand show.

Martha's Vineyard★★
7mi south of Hyannis. Access via ferry (see infobox below) or plane. Visitor information: Martha's Vineyard Chamber of Commerce on Beach Rd., Vineyard Haven; 508-693-0085 or 800-505-4815; www.mvy.com.

To Martha's Vineyard by Boat
The only line that accommodates cars and trucks, **Steamship Authority** *(508-477-8600; www.steamshipauthority.com)* offers ferry service from Woods Hole year-round daily to Oak Bluffs and Vineyard Haven. **Island Queen** *(508-548-4800; http://islandqueen.com)* offers seasonal daily walk-on, passenger-only service from Falmouth to Oak Bluffs. **Hy-line Cruises** *(800-492-8082; http://hylinecruises.com)* offers seasonal daily walk-on, passenger-only service from Hyannis to Oak Bluffs.

MUST SEE

What's With All the Grapes?

When Bartholomew Gosnold landed on the island in 1602, there were wild grapes growing all over the place. He pressed his beloved daughter's name in with the grape theme and Martha's Vineyard was born. Sadly, though the name stuck, the wild grapes have long since disappeared.

Actually, you'll find few vineyards on this triangular-shaped island, off the south coast of Cape Cod. You will find broad beaches, small fishing villages and summer resorts, shops, restaurants, attractions and the wildly popular **Mad Martha's** ice cream shop. The Vineyard population skyrockets in the summer, bringing a mix of day-trippers, vacationers and wealthy second-home owners.

Aquinnah Cliffs★★

Famous for their blue, tan, gray, red and orange hues, these 100-million-year-old clay cliffs contain fossils of prehistoric camels, wild horses and ancient whales. In summer, take a sunset tour ($5) of the 51-foot-high **Gay Head lighthouse** *(508-645-2300; http://gayheadlight.org).*

Edgartown★

Pleasure craft crowd Edgartown Harbor, once filled with whaling

vessels in the 19C. To get an idea of the town's past, visit the **Martha's Vineyard Museum** *(59 School St.; 508-627-4441; www. marthasvineyardhistory.org),* where historic houses showcase maritime and Native American artifacts.

Oak Bluffs★

In the 1830s the Methodists met in an oak grove here. Eventually some 12,000 people were attending annual services at **Cottage City** (later renamed Oak Bluffs). Today you can see the Victorian gingerbread cottages built to replace tents that stood near the tabernacle.

Then take a spin on the antique **Flying Horses Carousel** *(15 Lake Ave.; 508-693-9481; www. mvpreservation.org; open Jun–early Sept daily 10am–10pm; call for offseason hours; $2.50),* the oldest operating platform carousel in the country.

Aquinnah Cliffs

©Nick Tzolov/iStockphoto.com

CAPE COD AND THE ISLANDS

RESTAURANTS

Boston is legendary for its seafood, especially flavorful lobsters, succulent oysters, and meaty clams in chowder. City chophouses have been turning out hearty steaks for years. Yet today, international fare can be found here too, with gustatory options from refined French and Asian dishes to exotic Turkish foods and tasty Spanish tapas. Dining in Beantown has truly been, well, revolutionized.

Prices and Amenities

The venues below were selected for their ambience, location and/or value for money. Rates indicate the average cost of an appetizer, an entrée and a dessert for one person (not including tax, gratuity or beverages). Most restaurants are open daily, serve lunch and dinner (except where noted) and accept major credit cards. Call for information regarding reservations, dress code and opening hours. For a selected listing of restaurants by theme (Outdoor Dining, Star Chefs, etc.), see p138. Properties in this section are located in Boston unless otherwise noted.

Luxury	**$$$$**	**Over $50**
Expensive	**$$$**	**$30–$50**
Moderate	**$$**	**$15–$30**
Inexpensive	**$**	**Under $15**

BOSTON & CAMBRIDGE

Luxury

Asta
$$$$ New American
47 Massachusetts Ave. , Back Bay.
Dinner only. Closed Mon. 617-585-9575. www.astaboston.com.
Chef-owner Alex Crabb doesn't want people to have to think too hard about his menus, so he puts them together in 3, 5 and 8-course prix fixe options, plus extra cost

treats like foie-gras supplements and wine pairings. That way, diners can simply relax in this upscale bistro setting of brick walls and jazzy fabric banquettes and enjoy avant-garde recipes like warm oyster with oxtail in gastrique, beef heart with beets and tarragon, and a dainty cream puff decorated with black sesame and smoked maple.

Grill 23 & Bar
$$$$ American
161 Berkeley St., Back Bay.
617-542-2255. http://grill23.com.
Frequented by martini-quaffing power suits, this clubby Back Bay haven has welcomed expense-account customers for more than 20 years. The restaurant built its reputation on its top-quality steaks, but has also made its mark as a seafood destination. Preparations range from straightforward filet mignon, New York sirloin or grilled swordfish to more imaginative choices that might include tuna steak Diane with savory apple tart, root vegetable ragout and Madeira cream. The award-winning wine list spans 1,000-bottles strong, including nearly 30 wines by the glass and 75 half bottles.

Hamersley's Bistro
$$$$ French
553 Tremont St., South End.
Dinner & Sun brunch only.

617-423-2700.
www.hamersleysbistro.com.
Hamersley's helped establish
the South End as a prime dining
destination, and this petite
bistro, where patrons turn up in
everything from sweaters to suits,
is still going strong. The seasonal
menu, which features a variety
of local ingredients, stresses
creative comfort food with a
French flair, from its seared chicken
livers with polenta, black truffles
and Guinness Stout aioli, to the
signature garlicky roast chicken.
Hamersley's also make sure non-
meat eaters leave happy, with
vegetarian selections like roasted
sugar pumpkin stuffed with
Ancient grains, autumn vegetables
and braised greens in a spicy
Romesco sauce. Stop by in summer
for an al fresco bite on the patio.

Harvest
$$$$ New England
*44 Brattle St., Cambridge.
617-868-2255. www.harvest
cambridge.com.*
Fireplaces in the dining room and
on the patio considerably bump
up the already-warm feeling of
this Harvard Square favorite. The
landmark restaurant draws college
students when their parents are
in town, tweedy professorial
types who appreciate its subdued
elegance, and visiting foodies
from around the world. New
England bounty is served with
contemporary flair like Billi Bi
saffron mussel soup; Nantucket
Bay scallops atop squid ink risotto,
crimson carrots, cilantro and
tobiko; or herb crusted venison
over vanilla scented parsnip purée
with brussels sprouts, wheatberries
and red wine dried fig jus.

Hamersley's Bistro

©Matthew Demers/Hamersley's Bistro

Menton
♦♦♦♦   French/Italian
*354 Congress St., Waterfront.
Dinner only. 617-737-0099.
http://mentonboston.com.*
One of Boston's top tables, this
Relais & Châteaux dining room
offers fine dining, yet with a
modern interpretation of the
relaxed mood that today's patrons
demand. Skilled servers offer either
a four-course prix fixe menu, or
a more elaborate seven-course
chef's tasting menu with optional
wine pairings. Each course includes
multiple plate options: perhaps
baby octopus with Meyer lemon
brioche and lardo; red snapper
with cauliflower, lobster and
cranberry bean; or roasted game
hen with Chantenay carrots and
garlic brussels sprouts.

Rialto
$$$$ Italian
*In the Charles Hotel, One Bennett
St., Cambridge. Dinner only.
617-661-5050. www.rialto-
restaurant.com.*
Consistently ranked among the
Boston area's top restaurants,
Rialto serves up epicurean
elegance in a snazzy setting, with
striped lampshades and two-toned
wood floors complementing
curvaceous Art Deco-style seating

Rialto

and floor-to-ceiling windows. Chef Jody Adams' food derives its inspiration from southern Europe, updated with Boston panache: Expect savory seafood dishes, pastas and game prepared with seasonal vegetables and plated with artful precision. Save room for the rich honey ricotta cheesecake or experience an incredible take on pears, with crumbly almond cake dolloped in cinnamon cream, pear and ginger jam with pear sorbet and pomegranate seeds.

Expensive

Bristol Lounge
$$$ New American
200 Boylston St., in the Four Seasons Hotel, Back Bay. 617-338-4400. www.fourseasons.com.
The sophisticated bistro atmosphere of the Four Season's restaurant sets the scene nicely for upscale seafood and steak dishes where comfort foods like duck meatloaf also shine. Seasonal ingredients support signatures like golden Nantucket chowder stocked with blue crab and parsnips, or roasted baby

beet salad dotted with house made lemon ricotta, pumpkin seed brittle and blood orange reduction. It's worth showing up early so you'll have time for a drink in the restaurant's bar area, which offers a fine view of the Public Garden. On weekends, afternoon tea honors the Boston tradition dating back to 1773, with warm scones, tiny sandwiches and handcrafted pastries.

Beacon Hill Bistro
$$$ American/French
25 Charles St., Beacon Hill. 617-723-7575. www.beaconhillhotel.com/the-bistro.
Fear not, though the Beacon Hill Bistro is part of a hotel, it's in no way a *just-for-guests* establishment. The restaurant's modern white tablecloth-interior is accented with the warmth of wood and a gorgeous stained glass window behind the bar. Chef Joshua Lewin puts a modern spin on dishes, such as burnt lemon tagliatelle tossed with fried brussels sprouts, pumpkin seeds and (surprise) duck liver sauce, or duck breast that's cured in fennel, then paired with

Beacon Hill Bistro

© Brian Samuels/Beacon Hill Hotel and Bistro

butternut squash, duck confit, cranberry and puffed rye. The house-made charcuterie appetizer is a longtime hallmark of cured meats and terrines.

Durgin Park

$$$ New England
340 Faneuil Hall Marketplace, Downtown. 617-227-2038. www.arkrestaurants.com/ durgin_park.html.

For more than 130 years, Durgin-Park has been a Boston fixture, exuding a quirky charm, while serving slices of roast beef that are approximately the size of your head. Other hearty fare for which it is known includes shepherd's pie, corned beef and cabbage, Boston baked beans, and cornbread. Although the wait staff doesn't insult customers like they used to (well, as long as you don't annoy them first), they're hardly mellow. Nevertheless, diners sitting at the communal tables here enjoy the unpretentious food and bustling atmosphere.

Island Creek Oyster Bar

$$$ Seafood
500 Commonwealth Ave., in the Hotel Commonwealth, Kenmore Square. Dinner & Sun brunch only 617-532-5300. www.islandcreek oysterbar.com.

The seafood theme begins with the decor, including Gabion cages filled with thousands of Island Creek oyster shells. The menu pays homage to fish, and includes 18 kinds of oysters on the 25-seat bar that is divided by a raw seafood display. Since the food is fresh

© Michael Piazza

Island Creek Oyster Bar

daily, the sommelier offers a changing wine list to complement plates like Maryland Gold tilefish with ricotta gnocchi and black trumpet mushrooms, or bubbly rich seafood casserole. Steaks are also top-notch, as is the oven-roasted chicken zipped with sweet citrus and tart cranberry. Request a table in the main, industrial chic dining room if you're in a see and be-seen mood. For a quiet conversation spot, the smaller dining room is a better bet.

Jasper White's Summer Shack
$$$ **Seafood**
50 Dalton St., Back Bay; 617-867-9955. Also at 149 Alewife Brook Pkwy., Cambridge; 617-520-9500. www.summershackrestaurant.com.
Only a few chefs get over-the-title billing; Jasper White is one of them. He took the barnlike space of Aku Aku in Cambridge and turned it into a kitschy roadside diner, serving the likes of clambakes and corn dogs to rave reviews. The long lines attest to the popularity of the place, which gets the B52s-type ambience (lime-green booths, funky signage) and the menu just right. There's nothing "shacky" about the prices, but you do get that Jasperian touch, which elevates simple summertime fare to around-the-calendar delights.

Mamma Maria
$$$ **Italian**
3 North Square, North End. Dinner only. 617-523-0077. www.mammamaria.com.
Come here to enjoy neo-Italian food that isn't too, too nouveau. Mamma's does fish, braised meats and pasta with equal flair; think homemade dumplings filled with Maine lobster and hand-rolled pappardelle with rabbit, pancetta and rosemary. Lots of places come and go in the North End, but this one has stuck around and continues to make fans of first-time diners. The restaurant's location, in a 19C brick rowhouse that has played host to Italian restaurants since the 1960s, offers a tasty array of dining room choices, from the main-level spaces to more private second-floor spots that will make you feel like you're sharing a repast at a friend's house.

Sonsie
$$$ **International**
327 Newbury St., Back Bay. 617-351-2500. www.sonsieboston.com.
High-rent Newbury Street sports a number of cafes and outdoor eateries, but none is more popular (or versatile) than Sonsie. At lunch, white-aproned staff glide between the marble tables and wicker chairs to deliver homemade pastas, grilled sandwiches and brick-oven pizzas that supply the fuel needed for the day's shopping splurge. Dinner can be either casual in the cafe, where the floor-to-ceiling windows (folded back in summer) provide ample opportunities for people-watching, or more intimate in the restaurant, with its cozy booths, linen tablecloths and Mediterranean decor. And in true European style, the well-appointed bar serves everything from macchiatos to martinis all day long.

Toro
$$$ **Spanish Tapas**
1704 Washington St., South End. 617-536-4300. http://toro-restaurant.com. Brunch Sun.

Let's get this out of the way: Toro doesn't take reservations so, unless you get there early, you're going to wait.

Don't let that stop you. The wait is always worth it (and you might end up starting a great conversation that you can continue at the communal table inside). Chef Ken Oringer, who has several restaurants around the city (including Clio and Uni), has been getting rave reviews for his tapas from the day Toto opened. Request extra orders of the *gambas al ajillo* (griddled garlic shrimp)— they're too good to share.

Tremont 647
$$$ International
647 Tremont St., South End. Dinner & Sat–Sun brunch only. 617-266-4600. www.tremont647.com
Chef Andy Husbands borrows flavors from around the globe to create adventurous cuisine such as Korean dumplings, or tempura cod with yuzu aioli, kimchee vegetables and jasmine rice, alongside humble but delicious fried chicken. Art Deco chandeliers shaped like calla lily bouquets decorate the small dining room that draws a hip, must-wear-black crowd. The Sunday pajama brunch, when both staff and patrons show up in their nightclothes, is the next best thing to breakfast in bed.

T.W. Food
$$$ French
377 Walden St., Cambridge. Dinner & Sun brunch only. 617-864-4745. www.twfood restaurant.com.
Chef Tim Wiechmann trained in France, and uses Parisian inspiration for his cuisine classique updated with his own contemporary style. The white tablecloth fare is artfully arranged, but the setting, with weathered brick walls and comfy banquettes, is relaxed. Recipes can be complex, like sweetbread *cappelletti* with foie gras cream and black trumpet mushroom, but ordering is easy, thanks to prix fixe menus that range from three to seven courses.

Union Oyster House
$$$ Seafood
41 Union St., Downtown. 617-227-2750. www.unionoysterhouse.com.
Reputed to be America's oldest restaurant, this city staple was established way back in 1826. Daniel Webster was a regular in his day, and JFK slurped oysters here (see his booth in the upstairs dining room). You'll go for the historic appeal, but you'll fall for the pub-like atmosphere, and food like Boston scrod, haddock, sea scallops, and shrimp that's better than you'd expect. Grab a seat at the raw bar for a true Boston experience.

Union Oyster House

Union Oyster House

Moderate

75 Chestnut
$$ **American**
75 Chestnut St., Beacon Hill. Dinner & Sat–Sun brunch only. 617-227-2175. www.75chestnut.com.

This longtime classic destination off Charles Street is done in warm woods, brick and leather, with amber-glow lighting. Meals can start with seasonally flavored martinis, and end with an espresso martini alongside dessert. In between, the kitchen sends out expertly crafted signatures like herbed bacon clam chowder, hearty crab cakes, and a Porterhouse pork chop over New England mashed potatoes.

East Coast Grill & Raw Bar
$$ **American**
1271 Cambridge St., Cambridge. Dinner, Sat lunch & Sun brunch only. 617-491-6568. www.eastcoastgrill.net.

"Grills just want to have fun" is the theme at this Inman Square landmark, where crowds still gather for fresh grilled fish paired with flavor-loaded chutneys and salsas, and Southern-style barbecue. Chris Schlesinger's pulled-pork sandwiches are a messy plateful of heaven. Casual and noisy, it's cool for a crowd, but the dishes pack plenty of heat, especially on "Hell Nights" when area chili lovers gather to test their mettle (even the pasta is hellishly hot).

Finale
$$ **Desserts**
One Columbus Ave., Back Bay. 617-423-3184. Also at Harvard Square, 30 Dunster St., Cambridge; 617-441-9797. www.finale desserts.com.

Got a serious sweet tooth? Make tracks to this swanky dessert cafe, where the Theater District meets Back Bay. A hardcore sugar rush is guaranteed for those who dare order the sampler ($19.99), a tasting plate of ten mini desserts.

The Gallows
$$ **International**
1395 Washington St., South End. 617-425-0200. www.thegallows boston.com. No lunch Mon–Wed. Brunch Sun.

It's not often that a restaurant proudly proclaims that's it's "loud," but this eclectic neighborhood hot spot from owner Rebecca Roth also rightly boasts that it's "welcoming." Dark woods, muted lighting, a big bar and hip but friendly staff lend the backdrop to a far-reaching kitchen equally skilled with alentejana stew of Wellfleet clams, Berkshire pork, spicy tomato-garlic broth and crispy potatoes, as with pulled pork corn muffins dolloped in jalapeno pepper jelly, avocado and pickled red onion.

The Gallows

© The Gallows

Giacomo's
$$ **Italian**
*355 Hanover St., North End.
617-523-9026. Dinner only.
Also at 431 Columbus Ave.,
South End. 617-536-5723.
www. giacomosblog-boston.
blogspot.com. Cash only.*
If you're craving platters full of
red sauce and pasta, get on line
to—eventually—grab a table at
this perennial favorite. The friendly,
casual, cash-only restaurant serves
up simple, hearty fare at decent
prices. Warm up with the fried
calamari before moving on to the
salmon and sun-dried tomatoes In
tomato cream sauce over fettucine:
it's as good as it sounds.

Ginza
$$ **Japanese**
*16 Hudson St., Chinatown. 617-338-
2261. http://ginza-boston.com.*
Ginza serves up top-quality sushi
and sashimi. Also look for the
more modern maki rolls, like the
B-52 roll (yellowtail layered with
tempura) or the shaped-like-its-
name caterpillar maki. Those who
are sushi-shy will find plenty to fall
in love with at Ginza, including an
at-the-table stone grill where you
can fire up beef and seafood.

Legal Sea Foods
$$ **Seafood**
*26 Park Plaza, Back Bay. Check
online for other locations in the
Boston area. 617-426-4444.
www.legalseafoods.com.*
With branches around the city,
this seafood chain has been a local
favorite for more than 40 years. The
Park Square location is the flagship.
Legal Sea Foods serves some 20
varieties of fish each day, in a fresh,
straightforward manner. A few

menu items have an Asian edge,
like the tasty steamed mussels in a
fragrant seafood broth. The thick-
cut French fries are outstanding,
as is the clam chowder, served in
both calorie-dense creamy, and
light preparations.

New Shanghai
$$ **Chinese**
*21 Hudson St., Chinatown. 617-
338-6688. www.newshanghai
restaurant.com.*
Most restaurants in Boston's
Chinatown serve Cantonese-
style dishes, but New Shanghai
specializes In Shanghai-style fare.
The crispy scallops with black-
pepper sauce, the pan-fried rice
cakes (thick oval noodles sautéed
with meat, seafood or vegetables)
and the exotic braised eel are all
good choices. Lacquered chairs
and tropical fish tanks set it apart
from its modestly decorated
neighbors.

No Name Restaurant
$$ **Seafood**
*15½ Fish Pier, off Northern Ave.,
Seaport District. 617-338.7539.
www. nonamerestaurant.com.*
With no name and no nonsense,
this simple fish house near the
World Trade Center is a favorite of
in-the-know locals who don't mind
that the service is rather gruff—it's
all about the food here. You may
luck into a table in the back with a
harbor view. Yet don't worry if you
can't swing it. Once your chowder
and platters of fried fish arrive,
that's all you'll be able to focus
on anyway. Delicious healthier
broiled seafood is also available
but, seriously, you know what you
want to eat.

Warren Tavern

$$ **American**

2 Pleasant St., Charlestown. 617-241-8142. www.warrentavern.com.

With its low timbered ceilings, snug fireplace and long mahogany bar, this tavern may resemble an English pub, but in fact it's just as American as they come—Patriot, that is. Constructed c.1780, the structure was one of the first to be rebuilt after the British torched Charlestown in 1775. Doubling as a Masonic hall, the alehouse was a favorite of Paul Revere (whether the juicy Paul Revere Burger with sautéed mushrooms and Swiss has anything to do with the silversmith's culinary preferences is uncertain). George Washington was known to quaff a few here, too. Today Warren Tavern remains a cozy place for a cold Sam Adams beer and shepherd's pie (a house specialty), or hot chocolate by the fire after a long day on the Freedom Trail.

Inexpensive

Flour Bakery + Cafe

$ **Bakery/American**

12 Farnsworth St., Fort Point Channel. Check online for other locations in the Boston area. 617-338-4333. www.flourbakery.com.

It didn't take long for Flour to become a habit with many Bostonians. The bakery and cafe, which has expanded to four locations, is a pastry paradise— and the lunch fare, including sandwiches, salads and soups, will quickly become your daily must as well. Besides, Boston's a walking town so you're sure to work off your second and third cinnamon

Flour Bakery + Cafe

Flour Bakery + Cafe

cream brioche in no time. Flour's sweet interior offers plenty of seating, so get that rooibos tea latte to stay (after all, you need something to wash down yet another sticky bun).

Mr. Bartley's Burger Cottage

$ **American**

1246 Massachusetts Ave., Cambridge. Closed Sun. 617-354-6559. www.mrbartley.com. Cash only.

It's the juicy hamburgers, crisp onion rings and sweet-potato fries that entice hordes of students, locals and tourists to this bustling Harvard Square institution. Since 1961, Bartley's has offered a menu of burgers and frappes (that's milkshake, to you out-of-towners) that are fabulous. The burgers are named for famous (and infamous) politicians. Don't be afraid to cross party lines if a particular flavor combo appeals to you. Bring cash; Mr. Bartley's doesn't accept credit cards.

MUST EAT

The Paramount

$ **American**

44 Charles St., Beacon Hill. 617-720-1152. Also at 667 E. Broadway, South End. 617-269-9999. www.paramountboston.com

There's nothing stuffy about this Beacon Hill landmark, with its easy-on-the-pocketbook prices. This is the place where locals—and visitors in the know—head for hefty plates of bacon and eggs and steaming buttermilk pancakes in the morning, or freshly made sandwiches at lunchtime. But Paramount has a split personality. As evening approaches, the staff flips the lunchtime rules sign over to reveal a chalkboard where they write up the evening's specials. They dim the overheads, light candles, turn on the jazz, and delight dinners with still-reasonably priced table-service meals.

Sultan's Kitchen

$ **Turkish**

116 State St., Downtown. Closed Sun. No dinner Sat. 617-570-9009. www.sultans-kitchen.com.

A modest take-out spot with just a handful of tables, this tiny Turkish eatery is an excellent option for vegetarians or anyone looking for a fast, flavorful meal in the Financial District. The speedy staff will pack your choices to go, if you prefer to picnic at the waterfront, just a short walk away. Middle Eastern salads and sandwiches, including several types of kebabs, are featured, but be sure to leave room for a piece of the delightfully syrupy baklava.

Wichit

$ **American**

244 Newbury St., Back Bay. 857-277-1708. www.wichit sandwich.com.

The staff working at this classy brick and wood shrine to sandwiches are serious about their craft. Owners Chris and Rose Young focus on high end ingredients, and made-to-order signatures like the hearty combo of Stonemill NY strip, Swiss, Portabella, caramelized onions and roasted garlic aioli, all pressed hot on homemade rustic bread. Different sammys include spicy sushi tuna salad or chicken katsu.

Yankee Lobster Fish Market

$ **Seafood**

300 Northern Ave., Seaport District. 617-345-9799. www.yankeelobster company.com.

There's plenty of seafood to be had in Boston, but many locals who work in the Seaport/Fort Point Channel neighborhoods pick the usually packed Yankee Lobster as their top lunch spot. Get in line and start scanning the menu immediately—there's tons to choose from. Yankee definitely doesn't skimp on portions, so make sure you go hungry: once you start eating your order of fish and chips, or fish and calamari, or the seafood combo with scallops, you won't want to stop. The clam chowder is a no-brainer; you have to try it. The Zanti family, who own Yankee, have been fishing Boston's waters since the 1920s.

CAPE COD, MARTHA'S VINEYARD AND NANTUCKET

Restaurants listed in this section are open year-round and serve lunch and dinner unless otherwise noted.

Luxury

Alchemy

$$$$ New French
71 Main St., Edgartown, Martha's Vineyard. Call for winter hours. 508-627-9999.

White walls and white cloth-topped tables form the backdrop for the colorful French-inspired cuisine at this smartly casual two-level Edgartown bistro. Dinner entrées run the gamut from pan-roasted cod and lobster risotto to sirloin paired with "cheesy fondue." The lighter bar menu offers the likes of salmon cakes, Cuban sandwiches, and tequila-and-lime-glazed chicken. The curved, polished-wood bar draws year-'rounders and vacationers alike. It's a perfect place to imbibe a warming drink as the summer season gives way to cooler temps.

The Cape Sea Grille

$$$$ Seafood
31 Sea St., Harwich Port, Cape Cod. Closed Nov–mid-Apr. 508-432-4745. www.capeseagrille.com.

You don't have to love fish to eat here, but if you do, the contemporary seafood dishes are definitely worth a detour to Harwich Port. Filling an old sea captain's house, the dining rooms—with white tablecloths and captain's chairs—are not spacious. Better to focus on the food. The Cape Sea Grille's menu features innovative cooking that you won't see on the menu of every other restaurant on the

Cape. Recent choices include local Stoney Island mussels steamed in Cape Cod beer and peanut broth with roasted potatoes, red peppers, endive, red onions and ginger aioli, or oven-roasted local hake with roasted apple and Eastham turnip puree, sauté of braised endive, fennel confit and Swiss chard, finished in a roasted garlic-pomegranate broth. The apple cheddar cheesecake with Port caramel makes a decadent finale.

The Pearl

$$$$ Coastal Cuisine
12 Federal St., Nantucket. Dinner & Sat–Sun brunch only. Closed mid-Oct–Dec and Wed. 508-228-9701. www.boarding house-pearl.com.

The Asian-fusion dishes at this tony hot spot are as compelling and exotic as the tropical fish in the dining room's sparkling aquarium. From the yellowfin tuna martini to their signature dish, Nantucket salt-and-pepper wok-fried lobster, to the crispy Muscovy duck breast served with heirloom grain sushi rice and scallion pancake, the Pearl packs plenty of excitement onto its plates. The young, the adventurous, and the trust-fund-endowed all know this isn't just one of Nantucket's hottest see-and-be-seen spots; it's also one of substance.

The Pearl

© The Pearl

Òran Mór Bistro
$$$$ **Coastal Cuisine**
2 S Beach St, Nantucket. Dinner only. Closed Nov–late Apr. 508-228 8655. www.oranmorbistro.com.
An welcoming vision greets guests who ascend copper-clad stairs to the historic Nantucket home that's been transformed into an intimate bar and three dining rooms. Inside, the look is spare, with hardwood floors, simple gold-framed art, and a bartop covered with antique nautical drawings. Chef Chris Freeman and his wife Heather focus on local ingredients for nibbles like smoked local corn and housemade ricotta pierogies with beer-braised Vidalia onions and baked potato aioli, or entrées

such as sautéed sea scallops over BLT risotto studded with smoked bacon, arugula, cherry tomatoes and bottarga. Dessert is a must: the vanilla cream-filled brioche doughnuts with brown butter and roasted pear caramel, perhaps?

Sweet Life Café
$$$$ **New American**
63 Circuit Ave., Oak Bluffs, Martha's Vineyard. Dinner only. Closed Dec–Apr. 508-696-0200. www.sweetlifemv.com.
Choose a candlelit table inside this cozy Victorian house, whose romantic ambience lies worlds away from the hustle-bustle of Oak Bluffs. If you're going to pop the question on the Vineyard,

Òran Mór Bistro

© Kit Noble

this restaurant is the only one to consider. If the weather is fine, sit outside in the garden, which is lit by twinkling white lights. Inside or out, New American dishes like warm local littleneck clams and roasted bone marrow with fennel cream, sea beans and tobiko make the evening memorable.

Expensive

Black-Eyed Susans

$$$ **New American**

10 India St., Nantucket. Closed late Oct–early Mar and Sun. Breakfast and dinner only. 508-325-0308. www.black-eyedsusans.com. Cash only.

It looks like a luncheonette, but this unassuming spot boasts the island's best breakfast. Try the sourdough French toast slathered with orange Jack Daniels butter, or the spicy Thai scramble with Thai curry, broccoli, potatoes and cilantro. After the staff gets a chance to rest from the breakfast rush (and you've gotten enough sun), head back to Black-Eyed Susan's for dinner, when the lights are low and it takes on a more sophisticated (yet just as friendly) vibe. Evening options may include a wild salmon and bok-choy stir fry or five-spice pork on barley and edamame salad. Vegetarians will also find plenty to smile about on the menu, like an udon stir fry with tofu, rapini, pineapple and black-bean crumbs. Forget about charging it all; Black-Eyed Susan's is cash only.

The Black Dog

© The Black Dog

The Black Dog

$$$ **American/Seafood**

21 Beach St., Vineyard Haven, Martha's Vineyard. 508-693-9223. www.theblackdog.com.

You'll see Black Dog t-shirts long before you see the tavern. You might already own one. Open for more than four decades, The Black Dog (and the much-loved logo of the pup it was named for) isn't just a local favorite: it's become a nationally known brand. Luckily for hungry Vineyard visitors, it has stayed true to its roots and still serves up tasty fare from sun up to sun down. Start your day with a Red Hot Mama scrambled egg wrap, loaded with andouille sausage and jalapenos, and lay it to rest with a clam bake bucket for two or some deep fried oysters. Pick up cookies for the ferry ride home at the Black Dog Bakery *(11 Water St.)* And, of course, a t-shirt (or baseball cap or, for your Fido at home, a bandanna) . Now that you'll be able to say you actually ate at the Black Dog, you'll want to show your proof.

Centre Street Bistro

$$$ **New American**

29 Centre St., Nantucket. 508-228-8470, www.nantucketbistro.com.
Inventive food, a casual atmosphere, and moderate prices (for Nantucket) make this diminutive bistro worth a visit. The tiny dining room, with cheery yellow walls and floral-cushioned chairs, is a tight squeeze, but in mild weather you can sit outside on the patio. During a Nantucket winter, you'll probably welcome the extra body heat to help you shake off the outside chill. At lunch, owners Tim and Ruth Pitts offer intriguing salads, as well as new twists on old favorites, like a BLT with parmesan aioli and a cheeseburger in a flour tortilla with a side of potato pancake. Dinner follows the same contemporary direction: sesame-crusted shrimp gets a lively update with red curry rice noodles, crisp vegetables and mango relish, for example. They also serve a different risotto daily, and offer the bonus of being BYOB. For a sweet finish, the baked chocolate Marquis with butter pecan ice cream is required dining.

Sconset Café

Sconset Café

Sconset Café

$$$ **New American**

8 Main St., Post Office Square, Siasconset, Nantucket. Closed Oct–May. 508-257-4008. www.sconsetcafe.com. No credit cards.
In a simply-turned-out storefront on the island's east end, this contemporary nine-table cafe makes a relaxed spot for breakfast, lunch or dinner, far from the bustle of Nantucket village. The lunch menu features updated versions of classic sandwiches and salads; in the evenings, the fare runs to such dishes as crab cakes remoulade (a specialty here), and a Nantucket bouillabaisse rich with clams, mussels and halibut. The owners, who have had a connection to the island their entire lives, really understand all the elements of a perfect trip to Nantucket; that's why they opened a wine shop right next to the cafe that offers free corkage. Credits cards are not accepted, but cash or a check is welcome.

The Seafood Shanty

$$$ **Seafood**

31 Dock St., Edgartown, Martha's Vineyard. Closed mid-Oct–mid-May. 508-627-8622. www.theseafoodshanty.com.
Seats on the water? Check! Extensive menu of local seafood cooked almost any way you could want it? Check! Sushi made with fresh-as-fresh-can-be seafood? Check! And a kid's menu? Yes, it's true. The Seafood Shanty serves up a menu that makes it easy to satisfy everyone you're traveling with. With its wildly popular lobster quesadilla, the Shanty even puts a Mexican spin on the local catch. The menu features a serving

of prime rib so big that your most dedicated red meat-only family member will beg to come back here the next night.

Moderate

Bubala's by the Bay
$$ **New American**
183–85 Commercial St., Provincetown, Cape Cod. Closed Nov–Mar. 508-487-0773. www.bubalas.com.
A reasonably-priced option for Ptown, Bubala's isn't just a fun name, it's a fun (and tasty) place to eat. Regulars rely on the fish and chip, but the menu goes far beyond, with influences from all over the world. One night you can experience Caribbean flavors with West Indian-roasted lobster, and the next night, you can get a taste of Thailand with grilled chicken over sesame noodles and peanut dressing. The all-day breakfast menu is short, but, when you're offered buttermilk waffles with real maple syrup (it is New England after all) or huevos rancheros, what else could you need? Sit on the bay side for a fine waterfront view. Want to get an eyeful of all the action out on Commercial Street? There's plenty of seating on that side, too.

Fog Island Cafe
$$ **New American**
7 South Water St., Nantucket. Breakfast & lunch only. 508-228-1818. www.fogisland.com.
On Nantucket, even "down-home" is relatively upscale: witness this inviting cafe, with sturdy wooden tables, where owners Mark and Anne Dawson, graduates of the Culinary Institute of America,

serve up American comfort food with a contemporary edge. Throughout the year, it's a popular spot for breakfast (eggs, pancakes, breakfast sandwiches)—Fog-style chicken hash, loaded with red bliss potatoes, cream, eggs and much more, is a signature item. At lunch, a variety of soups (yes, New England clam chowder is always on the menu), burgers and wraps are served up. Other favorites include Nantucket fish cakes, build-your-own tacos, and a Cajun shrimp wrap. For dinner, visit the new sister property, **Fog Island Grille** nearby *(5 Amelia Dr.)*.

Inexpensive

Art Cliff Diner
$ **American**
39 Beach Rd., Vineyard Haven, Martha's Vineyard. Breakfast & lunch only. Closed Wed. 508-693-1224.
Although the open rafters and old-fashioned blue-and-white-checkered tablecloths would steer you to order plain old bacon and eggs or a burger and fries here, this diner's fare shows an innovative touch. Eggs might come in a chorizo frittata, waffles might be pumpkin-flavored, and lunch options encompass crispy fish tacos and grilled-eggplant sandwiches.

Cap'n Frosty's
$ **Seafood**
219 Main St. (Rte. 6A), Dennis, Cape Cod. Closed Labor Day–Mar. 508-385-8548. www.captain frosty.com.
Fried seafood is a Cape specialty, and this friendly clam shack has been doing a satisfying job of it for

Cap'n Frosty's

Cap'n Frosty's

more than 30 years. Choose among crispy-battered clams, scallops and other delicacies from the deep. Can't make up your mind? Get the Captain's Plate, stacked high with fish, clams, scallops and shrimp. Lobster roll fanatics will find their favorite here as well. Place your order at the counter, and then hunt for a seat at one of the Formica-topped tables in the bare-bones dining room. It's not a place to linger—there's no ambience and it's generally packed—but you can bring the kids and not worry about tracking in sand. Passing up a soft serve chocolate and vanilla swirl ice cream cone for dessert is, pretty much, an illegal act in Dennis, so don't even try it.

Mad Martha's
$ Ice Cream Shop
20 Union St., Vineyard Haven, Martha's Vineyard. Closed Oct–Apr. 508-693-5883. Cash only.
OK, so it's not technically a restaurant. But, on a summer vacation, nobody will quibble with you if you decide to have ice cream for lunch. Or dinner. Or breakfast. Luckily, this local legendary ice cream shop churns out enough flavors to keep you eating ice cream for a lifetime. Quite simply, a visit to Martha's Vineyard just isn't complete without (at least) one trip to Mad Martha's, but bring your greenbacks—it takes cash only.

Pie in the Sky Bakery
$ American
10 Water St., Woods Hole, Cape Cod. 508-540-5475. www.woodshole.com/pie.
Woods Hole residents are up and about early, between the marine center's activity and the constant arrival and departure of the Martha's Vineyard ferries at the Steamship Authority. So buy a newspaper and head for this pleasant cafe to enjoy coffee and breakfast fare. Even really early risers will fall for Pie in the Sky—which starts selling its organic Fair Trade in-house roasted coffee (and plenty of fresh-baked muffins and pastries as well) at 5am. Soups, salads and sandwiches—like The Vermonter, a heated ham, cheddar and apple extravaganza—are available for lunch and dinner. Sit inside or out on the little patio.

RESTAURANTS BY THEME

Looking for a restaurant with outdoor dining or a place to take the kids? In the preceding pages, we've organized the eateries by price category, so below we've broken them out by theme to help you plan your meals while you're in town. Restaurants are located in Boston, unless otherwise noted.

RESTAURANTS

HOTELS

Boston is a big city, yes. And it has big name high-rise hotels that have hundreds of rooms and all the latest amenities. But it also offers a variety of smaller lodgings that are equally comfortable, and cozy to boot, ranging from boutique hotels and inns to bed-and-breakfast accommodations. You're sure to find a place that fits your style as well as your budget.

Prices and Amenities

The properties listed below were selected for their ambience, locationand/or value for money. Price categories reflect the average cost for a standard double room for two people in high season, not including taxes or surcharges. High season in Boston is summer and fall (Jun–Oct); rates in Boston are usually lower in spring and winter. Many hotels on Cape Cod, Martha's Vineyard and Nantucket close in the winter months. Prices do not reflect the Boston hotel tax of 14.45% or the 11.7% lodging tax on Cape Cod and the islands. For a selected listing of lodgings by theme (Hotels with History, Posh Places, etc.), see p154. Properties are located in Boston unless otherwise noted.

Luxury	$$$$$	over $350
Expensive	$$$$	$250–$350
Moderate	$$$	$175–$250
Inexpensive	$$	$100–$175
Budget	$	Under $100

Luxury

Boston Harbor Hotel
$$$$$ 230 rooms
70 Rowes Wharf, Waterfront.
617-439-7000 or 800-752-7077.
www.bhh.com.
Overlooking Boston Harbor, this grand hotel—located across from the Financial District—boasts some of the city's best water views. The building's arched entry is one of Boston's most distinctive facades, and its location between the harbor and the Kennedy Greenway makes it an urban-outdoors lover's dream. The spacious guest rooms have marble baths as well as a home-like touch amid all the luxuries. Amenities include flat-panel plasma TVs, high-end bath products and custom-made leather desk accessories. Avail yourself of the many guest services, such as the nightly turndown. With windows facing the water, **The Meritage ($$$)** restaurant, showcases contemporary New England cuisine, wine pairings and small plates.

Boston Marriott Long Wharf
$$$$$ 412 rooms
296 State St., Waterfront.
617-227-0800 or 800-228-9290.
www.marriott.com.
A waterfront location, popular after-work bars, a public walkway and an open lobby make this large hotel a lively, integral part of the city's seaside scene. Most guest rooms have water views, and the property boasts an indoor pool and health club. It's super-convenient to waterfront attractions like the Boston Aquarium, Faneuil Hall and Boston Harbor boat trips and water taxis.

Four Seasons Hotel Boston
$$$$$ 273 rooms
200 Boylston St., Back Bay.
617-338-4400 or 800-332-3442.
www.fourseasons.com.
This grande dame, rising above
the Public Garden, has been a
favorite of well-heeled business
and pleasure travelers for more
than 20 years; it was extensively
modernized in 2006. Attentive
service is its hallmark, along with
generous on-site amenities like 24-
hour room service, free shoe shines
and complimentary town car
drop-off service. Considered one
of the top hotels in the world, the
Four Seasons offers well-appointed
rooms, and an 8th-floor swimming
pool with views of the State House.
After a martini there, enjoy duck
meatloaf or paella in the **Bristol
Lounge ($$$)**.

InterContinental Boston
$$$$$ 424 rooms
510 Atlantic Ave., Downtown.
617-747-1000 or 866-493-6495.
www.intercontinentalboston.com.
Harborside rooms may deliver an
incredible view of the Children's
Museum, but the look and vibe
of this luxury hotel are decidedly
adult. The lobby serves as a power-
meeting spot, and the rooms have
a strong masculine energy about
them. That's not to say there's no
warmth here. Far from it. There's a
coziness to the guest rooms (along
with very comfortable beds); the
deep bathtubs induce guests to
take a long soak after a day out.
The location—between the water
and the Kennedy Greenway—
makes it easy to get right into the
thick of the city. If you prefer a
night in, head to the lobby for a
drink at RumBa, a lively nightspot

beloved by out-of-towners and
locals alike, or an elegant meal at
Miel Brasserie Provencale ($$$).

The Liberty Hotel
$$$$$ 298 rooms
215 Charles St. 617-224-4000
or 800-325-3589. www.liberty
hotel.com.
The designers behind this
hotel, opened in 2007, are to be
congratulated. They played up the
theme of its historic building—the
19C Charles St. Jail—without
tipping into theme-park territory,
and they did it in remarkably
luxurious style. Stay in one of 18
guest rooms in the original jail
house or get an endless view of
Boston from the newer 16-floor
tower. Amenities include lush bath
products, flat-panel TVs and VoIP
telephones. Make sure you don't
take the key to your "personal
contraband" (also known as the
mini bar) with you when you leave
or they might make you come
right back. On second thought,
that would be just fine.

Nine Zero
$$$$$ 190 rooms
90 Tremont St., Downtown.
617-772-5800 or 866-906-9090.
www.ninezero.com.
One of Boston's finest boutique-
style hotels, this sleek and
stylish property, just off Boston
Common, is a favorite among
travelers looking for quiet, upscale
lodgings. The redbrick-and-
limestone facade is Old Boston, but
inside you'll find a contemporary
space, with plenty of glass, nickel,
chrome and steel. The effect is
serene; sink into fresh Frette linens,
pull up the goose-down comforter
and turn on the iPod music.

King Guest Room,
Ritz-Carlton, Boston Common

© Ritz-Carlton, Boston Common

Then wake up to a free overnight shoeshine, gratis use of your in-room yoga mat, and a tour around town on a complimentary bicycle.

Ritz-Carlton, Boston Common

$$$$$ **193 rooms**
10 Avery St., Beacon Hill.
617-574-7100 or 800-241-3333.
www.ritzcarlton.com.
If the words *modern* and *luxury* sum up your requirements for a hotel, book a room here. This contemporary glass-and-brick monolith boasts a $1 million modern art collection, sleek furnishings and legendary Ritz-style service. In 2008, an $11 million renovation of the guest rooms and public spaces pushed the look and comfort level of the already exceptional hotel into a new stratosphere. At this magnet for international travelers, guests who demand luxury in their workouts will be more than satisfied with an all-access pass to the 100,000-square-foot SportsClub/LA next door.

Expensive

Charles Hotel

$$$$ **294 rooms**
1 Bennett St., Cambridge.
617-864-1200 or 800-882-1818.
www.charleshotel.com.
Within walking distance of Harvard Square, this contemporary luxury hotel is a longtime favorite of Cambridge visitors. The modern exterior looks like a jumble of square and rectangular blocks, but done in the traditional red brick that echoes the Harvard campus. Inside, you'll find bright and airy rooms, simple four-poster beds and Shaker-style furniture. Cozy quilts and paintings add colorful accents. Dinner in **Rialto** *(see Must Eat)* is a must, and the **Regattabar** is a top haunt for jazz lovers *(see p 99)*. Guests can work out at the adjacent health club or, once the temps cool down, lace up their skates for the hotel's 2,900-square-foot outdoor ice rink.

Eliot Hotel

$$$$ **95 rooms**
370 Commonwealth Ave.,
Back Bay. 617-267-1607 or 800-443-5468. www.eliothotel.com.

MUST STAY

One of Back Bay's best values, this quiet, European-style boutique hotel, overlooking Commonwealth Avenue, features spacious suites, with living room, bedroom and kitchenette. French doors separate the bedroom from the living area, and antiques and floral fabrics decorate the spaces. Marble baths and antique reproductions add to the opulence. Amenities include cozy robes, fine-cotton bed linens, Internet access and 24-hour room service. The on-site, award-winning **Clio ($$$$)** restaurant is a favorite dining spot among Bostonians, as is **Uni ($$$)**, the Eliot's sashimi bar and lounge.

Fairmont Copley Plaza Hotel
$$$$ 383 rooms
138 St. James Ave., Back Bay.
617-267-5300 or 866-540-4417.
www.fairmont.com/copleyplaza.
Glamour and glitz are the operative words at the Fairmont's palatial property, the home base for visiting US presidents and foreign dignitaries since 1912. A look at the lobby's gilded coffered ceilings, crystal chandeliers and ornate French Renaissance-style furnishings may explain why Elizabeth Taylor and Richard Burton spent their second honeymoon here. In 2012, the property underwent extensive renovation showcasing blue and plum colors, plus customized black-and-white Boston portraits on the walls. The dark-paneled **Oak Long Bar & Kitchen** is a favorite spot for handcrafted cocktails alongside brasserie cuisine. In need of canine company in Boston? Take Catie and Carly Copley, the hotel's "canine ambassadors" out for a walk around town.

Hotel Marlowe
$$$$ 236 rooms
25 Edwin H. Land Blvd., Cambridge.
617-868-8000 or 800-825 7140.
www.hotelmarlowe.com.
This Kimpton property brims with bold colors and whimsical touches. Animal print carpeting meets gold and red-velvet fabrics and striped furniture in this lively venue. Rooms are spacious and a bit more soothing than the public areas, with neutral colors punctuated with colorful splashes. They have plenty of modern conveniences and amenities, like Frette bed linens, complimentary high-speed Internet access and an in-room exercise program. The nightly hosted wine hour, held in the small lobby area, is a hit with guests. Marlowe is also one of the pet-friendliest hotels in the area.

Loews Boston Hotel
$$$$ 225 rooms
350 Stuart St., Back Bay.
617-266-7200 or 855-495-6397.
www.loewshotels.com.
Located in the historic 1920s Boston Police Headquarters building, the 10-story property has been updated for modern

Lobby, Fairmont Copley Plaza Hotel

Fairmont Hotels and Resorts

HOTELS

conveniences without losing its gracious character. Inside, Old World charm meets modern style with a simple, almost serene, decor of neutral palettes, dark woods and traditional furnishings. Ambiance is friendly and casual, with an at-the-ready staff to help you.

Langham Hotel

$$$$ 318 rooms
250 Franklin St., Downtown.
617-451-1900 or 800-588-9141.
boston.langhamhotels.com.
Built in the 1920s to hold the Federal Reserve Bank of Boston, this dignified granite-and-limestone structure in the Financial District now houses a luxury hotel. Well-appointed rooms (with large, lighted closets, plush robes and make-up mirrors) possess distinctive features such as dramatic sloping windows with sweeping views. The hotel's Chuan Body + Soul spa *(see Spas)* offers treatments based on traditional Chinese medicine. One uber-popular spot is the Chocolate Bar at **Café Fleuri ($$):** the all-you-can-eat chocolate extravaganza *(Sat Sept–Jun)* is one of Boston's best date/anniversary locales.

Lenox Hotel

$$$$ 214 rooms
61 Exeter St. at Boylston St.,
Back Bay. 617-536-5300 or 800-
225-7676. www.lenoxhotel.com.
A Boston landmark, this historic property has been serving Boston dignitaries, celebrities and visitors since 1900. Family-owned since 1963, the Lenox prides itself in its over-the-top service. Beautifully restored in 2003, the hotel shows off public areas and rooms that gleam with dark woods, rich tapestries and rugs, and crystal and brass accents. Some corner rooms have wood-burning fireplaces; others boast views of Back Bay and the Charles River. Its location, within walking distance of Newbury Street shops and restaurants, is an added plus.

Omni Parker House

$$$$ 551 rooms
60 School St., Downtown.
617-227-8600 or 888-444-6664.
www.omnihotels.com.
The oldest continuously operating hotel in the country, this city landmark faces Boston Common at the foot of Beacon Hill. Expect hushed, Brahmin-style elegance:

Langham Hotel

© Gwen Cannon/Michelin

Deluxe Guest Room, Taj Boston

© Taj Hotels Resorts and Palaces

wood paneled walls, jewel-colored fabrics, brass elevator doors, low lights and cherry wood furniture. Rooms are smallish but comfortable, and as part of a $30 million renovation in 2008, have been updated with high-tech conveniences like flat-screen LCD televisions. Upstart John F. Kennedy announced his first campaign for public office here. Parker House Rolls and Boston Cream Pie were both born here. Today you can sample them at **Parker's ($$$)** Restaurant.

Onyx Hotel
$$$$ **112 rooms**
155 Portland St., Downtown.
617-557-9955 or 866-660-6699.
www.onyxhotel.com.
Artsy and sexy describe this boutique hotel, located in the revitalized Bullfinch Triangle, three blocks from North Station. You'll be dazzled by the first thing you'll see: the luscious, newly renovated Ruby Room, with its curvy lines, deep-red fabrics, black-granite bar (with fiber optics to make your drinks twinkle!), and great Ruby burgers, too. The flash—think black and white and red splashes

of color against a neutral taupe backdrop—continues throughout the tiny lobby and good-size rooms.

Taj Boston
$$$$ **273 rooms**
15 Arlington St., Back Bay.
617-536-5700 or 877-482-5267.
www.tajhotels.com.
The Taj Boston had a big bed to fill when it took over the space from the Ritz-Carlton in 2007. So far it's definitely been equal to the task. Owned by a luxury hotel chain with properties in 17 countries, the hotel is housed in a landmark building overlooking the Public Garden *(see Parks & Gardens)*. Shoppers bent on hitting the city's upscale boutiques will appreciate the Taj's location, on the corner of Newbury and Arlington. During Boston's blustery winters, push the hotel's already-warm ambience over-the-top in a suite with a wood-burning fireplace. The Fireplace Butler will get the flames going for you, with your choice of wood. For an elegant break, enjoy afternoon tea in The Lounge, a tradition here since 1927.

Westin Copley Place
$$$$ **803 rooms**
10 Huntington Ave., Copley Place, Back Bay. 617-262-9600 or 888-625-5144. www.westincopley placeboston.com.
This gleaming glass-and-steel high rise sits in busy Copley Place with skywalk access to Copley Place and Prudential Center shops. The 36-story hotel draws hordes of business travelers and conventioneers who like the Back Bay location and can afford the higher prices. Rooms are done in earth tones with comfy beds and in-room coffeepots equipped with Starbucks coffee. Bar 10 restaurant ($$) offers upscale American bistro cuisine in a lounge setting; the lobster mac 'n' cheese is a favorite.

XV Beacon
$$$$ **60 rooms/3 suites**
15 Beacon St., Beacon Hill. 617-670-1500 or 877-982-3226 www.xvbeacon.com.
Unsurpassed luxury is what you'll find at this Beacon Hill hotel. The Beaux-Arts building's original 1903 cage elevator whisks guests up to oversize rooms outfitted with canopy beds, working gas fireplaces and mahogany paneling. Amenities include personalized butler service (even for canine guests), complimentary in-town chauffeured Lexus sedan service, and in-room gadgets like four-inch LCD TVs in the bathroom and surround-sound stereo. The in-hotel steakhouse, **Mooo ($$$$)**, may have a playful name, but it serves seriously good eats.

Beacon Hill Hotel and Bistro

Moderate

Beacon Hill Hotel and Bistro
$$$ **13 rooms**
25 Charles St., Beacon Hill. 617-723-7575 or 888-959-2442. www.beaconhillhotel.com.
If the weather is mild, slip up to the roof terrace at this swank small hotel on Beacon Hill's main street to sip a glass of wine and watch the world go by. Like the terrace, the entire property feels like a stylish urban oasis. Rooms are sleek, almost spare, sporting fluffy duvets and hi-tech flat-screen TVs. Rates include a full breakfast in the Parisian-style bistro, which also serves high-quality French cuisine at lunch and dinner *(see Must Eat)*.

Clarendon Square Inn
$$$ **3 rooms**
198 W. Brookline St., South End. 617-536-2229. www.clarendon square.com.
This South End brownstone is stylishly appointed with a mix of Victorian antiques and contemporary designer touches. Modern art adorns the parlor walls, and marble mantels surround the fireplaces. Hotel-type amenities—complimentary Wi-Fi, voice-mail service, hair dryers, a

guest refrigerator—abound, and continental breakfast is served in the dining room. Soak away stress in the rooftop hot tub.

Copley Inn
$$$ **20 rooms**
19 Garrison St., Back Bay. 617-236-0300. www.copleyinn.com.
Reasonable prices and a central location—just behind the Prudential Center—are the strengths of this modest inn. Contained in a four-story brownstone (note that there is no elevator), the rooms are neat, if rather basic (think motel-style Victorian reproductions), but all have kitchenettes. For Old Boston charm and a little more space, request one of the large bowfront rooms with a bay window.

Encore
$$$ **4 rooms**
116 West Newton St., South End. 617-247-3425. www.encore bandb.com.
A quiet alternative to large convention hotels, this small, classy B&B in the now-trendy South End has four individually decorated guest rooms. Natural light abounds in the contemporary-style rooms, each with private bath and queen-size bed. The design is sleek, with brick accent walls, wood beams, and streamlined furnishings done in shades of green, brown and purple. A stay at the renovated 19C town house also includes a continental breakfast—and Boston skyline views.

Harborside Inn
$$$ **116 rooms**
185 State St., Waterfront. 617-723-7500. www.harborsideinn boston.com.
Looking for a great location, a historic property and a good value all in one? Check out this hotel in the Financial District, just steps from Faneuil Hall, Quincy Marketplace and the waterfront. Rooms in this converted 1846 mercantile warehouse are charmingly decorated with teak woodwork, imported Italian tile and nautical lighting fixtures.

Hotel Commonwealth
$$$ **150 rooms**
500 Commonwealth Ave., Back Bay. 617-933-5000 or 866-784-4000. www.hotel commonwealth.com.
This independently owned luxury property overlooks Kenmore Square, an area that has been transformed from gritty to gorgeous over the last few years. There are two styles of rooms: one with a view of Fenway Park (popular with zealous Red Sox fans) that feature a small sitting area; the other is slightly larger (an additional 30 square feet) with views of Commonwealth Avenue. All have writing desks, marble baths, flat-screen TVs, DVD players, and high-speed Internet access.

Albee Room, Encore
© Encore

HOTELS

147

John Jeffries House

$$$ **46 rooms**

14 David G. Mugar Way at Charles Circle, Beacon Hill. 617-367-1866. www.johnjeffrieshouse.com.

Sitting at the foot of Beacon Hill, this solid-looking, four-story redbrick building, built in the early 1900s, lies opposite a bustling traffic circle and the Charles Street T station. Despite its location, the inside is surprisingly serene. Well-maintained rooms are furnished with period reproductions, and most have kitchen facilities. Although the guest rooms are not large, many have separate sitting areas. Enjoy a continental breakfast in the large parlor, which offers views of the Charles River.

Mary Prentiss Inn

$$$ **20 rooms**

6 Prentiss St., Cambridge. 617-661-2929. http://maryprentissinn.com.

Situated on a narrow residential street between Harvard and Porter squares, this 1843 Greek Revival-style mansion is the setting for an inviting bed-and-breakfast inn. Mixing traditional and modern, it's attractively furnished with Victorian-era antiques like wing-back chairs and four-poster beds; contemporary comforts include rooms with fireplaces, whirlpool tubs, wet bars and refrigerators. All rooms have private bathrooms. A full breakfast and afternoon tea are included in the rate.

Millennium Bostonian Hotel

$$$ **201 rooms**

26 North St. at Faneuil Hall, Downtown. 617-523-3600. www.milleniumhotels.com.

If you like to be in the middle of the action, you can't beat this European-style hotel at bustling Faneuil Hall Marketplace. A stunning steel sculpture and a fountain greet guests at the cobblestone rotary outside the check-in area; the lobby sits beneath a soaring atrium of glass and steel. Rooms in the older wing, a converted 1824 warehouse, feature high ceilings, tall windows, wooden beams, exposed brick walls and working fireplaces. New-wing rooms sport a sleek design with wood paneling. Some rooms have balconies overlooking Faneuil Hall or the North End. North 26 restaurant and bar sits on-site, and the full-service salon and day spa lies adjacent.

Newbury Guest House

$$$ **32 rooms**

261 Newbury St., Back Bay. 617-670-6000 or 800-437-7668. www.newburyguesthouse.com.

Set on Boston's prime shopping street, this lodging, comprising three attached 1880s brownstones, makes an excellent value for the neighborhood. It's close enough to the Hynes Convention Center and the many Back Bay corporate offices to draw both business travelers and vacationers. Rooms, some with bay windows, are furnished with Victorian-style reproductions and Oriental rugs.

Seaport Hotel

$$$ **426 rooms**

One Seaport Lane, South Boston. 617-385-4000 or 800-440-3318. www.seaportboston.com.

While its location next to the Seaport World Trade Center has long made this hotel a magnet for conventioneers, its new nearby neighbor, the Institute of

Contemporary Art *(see Museums)*, has turned the Seaport Hotel Into a convenient lodging for art lovers as well. Whether you're in town for business or pleasure, request a high-up room with (depending on your taste) a view of either the Boston Harbor or the city skyline. The on-site fitness center, with spa services, is a beneficial amenity. It's also a great place for families; the large indoor pool is always an instant favorite of kids and the Seaport's restaurant, **Aura** **($$$$)**, caters to wee ones with an extensive children's menu.

Inexpensive

A Cambridge House Inn
$$ 15 rooms
2218 Massachusetts Ave., Cambridge. 617-491-6300 or 800-232-9989. www.acambridge house.com.
This well maintained turn-of-the-19C Victorian house is filled with patterned fabrics, four-poster and iron beds and comfortable furnishings. Rooms are spacious, some with working fireplaces, all with private baths, high-speed Internet access and cable TV.

A Cambridge House Bed & Breakfast Inn

Although it's located on busy Massachusetts Avenue, minutes from Harvard Square, the house sits back from the road, and once inside, it's nice and quiet. A continental breakfast is served.

Chandler Inn Hotel
$$ 55 rooms
26 Chandler St., South End. 617-482-3450 or 800-842-3450. www.chandlerinn.com.
You'll get great value at this casual, friendly hotel in the lively, revitalized South End. The eight-story high rise is within walking distance of Back Bay shopping and dining, and an easy subway ride to citywide attractions. Though the hotel has long been known for its simply furnished rooms, guests now have an option. Rooms have been given a designer overhaul and are loaded with the in-room amenities boutique hotel fans have come to expect, like marble baths and flat screen satellite TVs.

Budget

40 Berkeley Hostel
$ 20 rooms
40 Berkeley St., South End. 617-375-2524. www.40berkeley.com.
It's a hostel, but all the modern rooms are private, Wi-Fi and breakfast are free, and the location is unbeatable: it's a walkable distance to Back Bay, Copley Square, and Boston Commons. A hip dinner cafe, billiards tables, fireplace parlor and housekeeping services make the place a steal.

STAYING ON CAPE COD, MARTHA'S VINEYARD AND NANTUCKET

Properties listed in this section are open year-round, unless otherwise noted.

Luxury

Hob Knob

$$$$$ 17 rooms, 2 houses
128 Main St., Edgartown, on Martha's Vineyard. 508-627-9510 or 800-696-2723. www.hobknob.com.
Overlooking historic Edgartown, this eco-conscious inn is filled with antiques, fresh flowers and a friendly staff. Rooms are drenched in light, with floral fabrics, crisp white linens and comforters, and fluffy down pillows. To fully experience the Vineyard, rent one of the hotel's beach-cruiser bikes or take a sunset cruise on the Hob Knob's 27-foot Boston Whaler (and, yes, it comes with a captain and crew so you can just sit back and watch the water).

The Wauwinet

$$$$$ 32 rooms, 4 cottages
120 Wauwinet Rd., Nantucket. 508-228-0145 or 800-426-8718. www.wauwinet.com. Closed late Oct–early May.

The Wauwinet

© Nantucket Island Resorts

Arguably the finest place to stay on the island, this private, pristine property abuts the Great Point Wildlife Sanctuary, overlooking waves of sea grasses, rolling dunes and the waters of Nantucket Bay. The serene and luxurious resort, nine miles from town, offers a multitude of daily activities, like mountain biking, croquet, tennis, nature hikes, cruises, boating and fishing. It's consistently ranked as one of the top beach hotels in the country, and the resort's **Toppers** (**$$$$**) restaurant ranks among the island's finest. Wauwinet boasts an on-property spa, too, so now there's absolutely no reason to leave.

White Elephant

$$$$$ 53 rooms, 11 cottages
50 Easton St., Nantucket. 508-228-2500 or 800-445-6574. www.whiteelephanthotel.com. Closed mid-Dec–late Apr.
Whitewashed walls and woodwork, crisp linens, wicker furniture, and sweeping harbor views grace this Nantucket landmark. Reeking of casual elegance, the sprawling gray-shingled beach hotel has been a top address for island visitors since the 1920s. Nantucket's shops, museums and restaurants are just a short walk away. Expect attentive service, Old-World civilities (an afternoon port and cheese reception) and modern amenities like high-speed Internet access, in-room spa treatments and a 24-hour concierge. Traveling with a small

White Elephant

group? Consider the three-bedroom White Elephant Loft, which accommodates up to eight people—and is perfect for families with kids.

Expensive

Brass Key Guesthouse
$$$$ **42 rooms**
67 Bradford St., Provincetown, on Cape Cod. 508-487-9005 or 800-842-9858. www.brasskey.com. Closed early Nov–Mar.
You'll need to book far in advance for a high-season stay at this guesthouse in bustling Provincetown. The property consists of five 18C and 19C houses and three cottages, clustered around gardens and a pool. Spacious rooms are individually decorated with period decor and

Brass Key Guesthouse

antique furnishings; beds sport luxurious linens and goose-down pillows. Some rooms even have fireplaces, whirlpool tubs, heated towel racks and private decks. The compound sits on a quiet side street, within walking minutes to the hub of P-Town activity.

Captain's House Inn
$$$$ **16 rooms**
369-377 Old Harbor Rd., Chatham, on Cape Cod. 508-945-0127 or 800-315-0728. www.captainshouseinn.com.
It's hard to imagine a more romantic place to stay on the Cape than this long-time favorite lodging in Chatham. Consisting of an 1839 Greek Revival home, carriage house and renovated stables, the Captain's House features deluxe rooms, most with canopied beds, fireplaces, double whirlpool baths and modern amenities (Internet access, flat-screen TVs, CD players). There are plenty of public spaces, too; cuddle up next to the fireplace in the sitting room, or relax in the vintage library. Rooms are filled with comfy chairs, period antiques and quality reproductions. In need of some pampering? Ask the front desk to set up an in-room massage for you.

HOTELS

Dockside Inn

$$$$ 21 rooms

9 Circuit Ave., Oak Bluffs,
on Martha's Vineyard. 508-693-
2966 or 800-245-5979.
www.vineyardinns.com.
Closed late Oct–early May.
Completely renovated in 2012,
this harbor district property
boasts a dramatic contemporary
design, with crisp lines, swanky
furnishings, and palettes of bright
blue, silver and wood. Many
rooms command views of the
water and Ocean Park. Service hits
high luxury notes, including free
afternoon cookies, ice cream in the
summer, and a Rolls Royce Silver
Cloud as the courtesy car.

Jared Coffin House

$$$$ 43 rooms

29 Broad St., Nantucket. 508-228-
2400. www.jaredcoffinhouse.com.
You can't miss this three-story
1845 brick mansion in the center
of town. If you like staying
in impeccably restored and
maintained historic hotels, this is
the place for you. There's a wide
range of room options at this hotel
in Nantucket's quaint historic
district . All offer colonial charm,
some with canopied beds, working
fireplaces and Oriental rugs. The
friendly staff at this sister property
of the White Elephant can help you
plan the perfect day, including a
visit to the White Elephant Spa.

Mansion House

$$$$ 40 rooms

9 Main St., Vineyard Haven,
on Martha's Vineyard. 508-693-
2200 or 800-332-4112.
www.mvmansionhouse.com.
After a day exploring Martha's
Vineyard, poking around shops,
biking and beaching, the full-
service spa at the Mansion House
is a welcome retreat. Relax with
a mud body wrap or a massage,
join a yoga class, or just relax in
the mineral spring pool or sauna.
The 5,000-square-foot spa and
fitness center is a major draw for
this Vineyard Haven property, as
are the spacious rooms, friendly
owners, and health club with a
"spring water" pool. A $10-million
restoration project was completed
in 2003, after a fire swept the
historic 1794 hotel. Today, it
remains a landmark and favorite
among island locals and
visitors alike.

Orleans Waterfront Inn

$$$$ 11 rooms

3 Old County Rd., Orleans,
on Cape Cod. 508-255-2222
or 800-863-3039.
www.orleansinn.com.
This 1875 former sea captain's
home brims with Victorian charm,
offering rooms that are cheery,
and bright with floral prints and
country furnishings. Its waterfront
location, in desirable Orleans, is
tough to beat, and if a view of
the water is a must, make sure
to reserve one of the rooms that
overlooks Town Cove. Some

Orleans Waterfront Inn

Orleans Waterfront Inn

MUST STAY

rooms have working fireplaces to take the chill off end-of-season stays. Guests have access to the inn's kitchenette area and the waterfront deck, a popular place to relax. A complimentary breakfast is a welcome addition.

Moderate

The Beachside
$$$ 90 rooms
30 North Beach St., Nantucket. 508-228-2241 or 800-322 4433. www.thebeachside.com. Closed late Oct–early May.
Families love this quiet motel-style property, a five-minute walk from the kid-friendly Jetties Beach. Up for a post-beach ice cream? It's just a short stroll to historic Main Street. Rooms are clean, bright, and airy and come with a small refrigerator and cable TV. There's an outdoor pool and a free continental breakfast. Families who decide to bring Fido along can book a pet-friendly room for an additional charge. If you prefer the beach after the summer crowds scatter, call to find out about fall getaway packages.

Captain Freeman Inn
$$$ 11 rooms
15 Breakwater St., Brewster, on Cape Cod. 508-896-7481 or 855-896-7481. www.captain freemaninn.com.
Loyal guests have been happy to see that this inn on the Outer Cape hasn't change much after new owners took it over in 2011. The wine and beer bar they added is much-loved. The immaculately kept inn features a wrap-around porch, and spacious guest rooms decorated with canopied beds,

Captain Freeman Inn

Captain Freeman Inn

country lace, and floral fabrics and wallcoverings. Flower and herb gardens surround the outdoor pool area, and it's just a short walk to Breakwater Beach on Cape Cod Bay. The seven Deluxe Rooms come equipped with two-person whirlpool tubs and fireplaces. Children ages 10 and older are welcome. Cooks take note: the inn offers culinary classes during the winter and spring months.

Inexpensive

Seacoast Inn
$$ 26 rooms
33 Ocean St., Hyannis. 508-775-3828. www.seacoastcapecod.com. Closed late-Oct–Apr.
Renovated floor-to-ceiling in 2010, this modern motel-style lodging has simple but spotless accommodations. Rooms feature updated decor, free Wi-Fi and cable TV. A continental breakfast is included in the rate. The location is great, near Main Street of central downtown Hyannis, with easy ferry access to the islands of Nantucket and Martha's Vineyard.

HOTELS

HOTELS BY THEME

Looking for the best business hotels in Boston? The best hotels to take tea? Want to bring Fido along? In the preceding pages, we've organized the properties by price category, so below we've broken them out by theme to help you plan your trip. Hotels are in Boston, unless otherwise noted.

Best Places to Really Get Away

Closest Hotels to Fenway Park

Close to Public Parks

For College Students' Parents—Boston

For College Student's Parents—Cambridge

Easy on the Budget

For Business Travelers

For Families

MUST STAY

HOTELS

BOSTON

INDEX

INDEX

157

List of Maps

Photo Credits (page Icons)
Must Know
©Blackred/iStockphoto.com *Star Attractions:* 6-9
©Nigel Carse/iStockphoto.com *Calendar of Events:* 10-11
©Richard Cano/iStockphoto.com *Practical Information:* 12-21
Must Sees
Greater Boston CVB/FayoFoto, Inc. *Neighborhoods:* 24-35, *Cambridge:* 36-39, *Historic Sites:* 40-47, *Landmarks:* 48-55, *Parks & Gardens:* 64-69
©Terraxplorer/iStockphoto.com *Museums:* 56-63

Must Dos
Greater Boston CVB/FayFoto, Inc. *Fun:* 70-77
©Michael Walker/iStockphoto.com *Kids:* 78-84
©Shannon Workman/Bigstockphoto.com *Performing Arts:* 85-89
©Alex Slobodkin/iStockphoto.com *Shop:* 90-95
©Jill Chen/iStockphoto.com *Nightlife:* 96-99
©ImageDJ *Spas:* 100-101
©Kutt Niinepuu/Dreamstime.com *Best Excursions from Boston:* 102-121
©Marie-France Bélanger/iStockphoto.com *Restaurants:* 122-139
©Larry Roberg/iStockphoto.com *Hotels:* 140-155

INDEX